Praise for *Cri.*

MW00774118

"With insightful analysis and crystalline reporting, Robert Kimball gives the lie to the notion that the Civil Rights Act was solely the result of White House management and Democratic energy. Republican leaders like Charlie Halleck and William McCulloch get their due, but so do countless lesser-known politicians and staff members who worked tirelessly to bring this landmark legislation to life."

—**Clay Risen,** author of *The Bill of the Century: The Epic Battle for the Civil Rights Act*

"Far more than a memoir, Robert Kimball's *Crisis and Compromise* traces in step-by-step detail the congressional maneuvers, backroom negotiations, betrayals, personalities, and emotions that gave birth to the 1964 Civil Rights Act. Told from the perspective of a young and eager congressional aid intimately involved in the process, Kimball refocuses the familiar narrative to highlight the seldom acknowledged—but central—role liberal and moderate Republicans played in passing the most important legislative act of the 20th century. Along with some surprising, revealing, and amusing stories about well-known participants in the process, Kimball's book is especially valuable at a time when bipartisanship appears to be a forgotten practice."

—**Arlene W. Saxonhouse,** Caroline Robbins Professor of Political Science, Emerita University of Michigan

"It seems unlikely that a story about the congressional journey of a bill would be a cliff-hanger, but Robert Kimball's memoir will keep you turning the pages even though you know the legislation will become law in the end. Not just any law, of course, but the Civil Rights Act of 1964. In this important, first-person chronicle about his experience working on the historic, bipartisan legislation as a staffer for Republicans in the House of Representatives, Kimball delivers a message that should be instructive to members of both parties in Congress today."

—Joseph I. Lieberman,
United States Senator from Connecticut (1989-1913)

"Robert Kimball's memoir is a riveting revelation of the legislative maneuvering over the bill that would become the Civil Rights Act of 1964, the most important civil rights law in American history. As a recent Yale college graduate in the fall of 1963, Kimball played a key role behind the scenes in the deal-making that rescued a bill seemingly headed for defeat. Based on contemporaneous notes and files, this previously untold story is a significant contribution to the history of legislative and party politics in an era when, despite the noise of partisanship, compromise was possible."

—Jethro K. Lieberman, author of *The Litigious Society* and other books on the American legal system

"This stirring first person account of the negotiations to get the Civil Rights Act of 1964 through the U.S. House of Representatives sheds light on one of the most crucial moments in congressional history. Robert Kimball, as a Republican aide, participated in the action and now has recorded it. This book is a must read for students of the Civil Rights Act of 1964, congressional history, and leadership in action."

—Robert D. Loevy, editor of *The Civil Rights Act of 1964: The Passage of the Law That Ended Racial Segregation*; Emeritus Professor of Political Science, Colorado College

CRISIS

AND

COMPROMISE

THE RESCUE OF THE
1964 CIVIL RIGHTS ACT

A MEMOIR

ROBERT KIMBALL

RIVER GROVE
BOOKS

This book is a memoir reflecting the author's present recollections of experiences over time. The words, except otherwise noted, and the story are the author's alone. Some details and characteristics may have changed, some events may have been compressed, and some dialogue may have been recreated.

Published by River Grove Books
Austin, TX
www.rivergrovebooks.com

Distributed by River Grove Books

Design and composition by Greenleaf Book Group and Sheila Parr
Cover design by Greenleaf Book Group and Sheila Parr

Grateful acknowledgment is made to the following sources for permission to reproduce copyrighted material.

From "The Congress: Where Are We At Here?" by Ronald Libonati from *TIME* magazine, November 1, 1963. Copyright © 1963 TIME USA LLC. All rights reserved. Used under license.
http://content.time.com/time/subscriber/article/0,33009,875291,00.html

From "Congress Faces Crucial Decision on Civil Rights" by Anthony Lewis from the *New York Times*, October 28, 1963. Copyright © 1963 The New York Times Company. All rights reserved. Used under license.
https://www.nytimes.com/1963/10/28/archives/congress-faces-crucial-decision
-on-civil-rights-house-panel-acts.html

From "Rights Bill Move Set For January" by E.W. Kenworthy from *The New York Times*, December 6,1963. Copyright © 1963 the New York Times Company. All rights reserved. Used under license.
https://www.nytimes.com/1963/12/06/archives/rights-bill-move-set-for
-january-smith-promises-action-by-house.html

Publisher's Cataloging-in-Publication data is available.

Print ISBN: 978-1-63299-414-1

eBook ISBN: 978-1-63299-415-8

First Edition

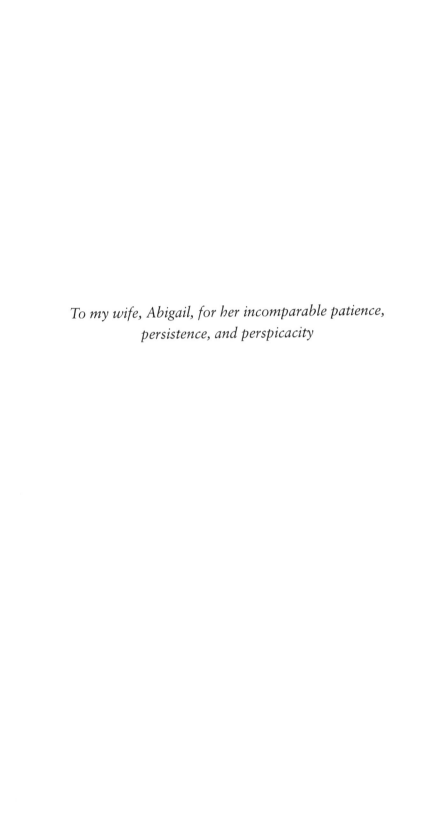

To my wife, Abigail, for her incomparable patience, persistence, and perspicacity

I go for honorable compromise whenever it can be made. Life itself is but a compromise between life and death, the struggle continuing throughout our whole existence, until the great Destroyer finally triumphs. All legislation, all government, all society, is formed upon the principle of mutual concession, politeness, comity, courtesy; upon these, everything is based.

—Henry Clay
During the debate in the United States
Senate on the Compromise of 1850
April 8, 1850

Early in life I had noticed that no event is ever correctly reported in a newspaper, but in Spain, for the first time, I saw newspaper reports which did not bear any relation to the facts, not even the relationship that is implied in an ordinary lie. . . . This kind of thing is frightening to me, because it often gives me the feeling that the very concept of objective truth is fading out of the world. . . . I am willing to believe that history is for the most part inaccurate and biased, but what is peculiar to our age is the abandonment of the idea that history could be truthfully written.

—George Orwell
Looking Back on the Spanish Civil War (1943)

Few people will believe that the Republicans played such an important role in passing the civil rights bill. Someone needs to tell our story.

—Representative Charles Halleck
(R-Indiana) to the author
Fall 1963

Contents

September 1962: Representative Thomas Curtis (R-Missouri) devises a strategy to help defeat the Industrial Security Bill, the first time the House Un-American Activities Committee is rebuffed in the United States House of Representatives.

Fall 1962: Republicans on the House of Representatives Judiciary Committee start drafting a comprehensive civil rights bill.

January 14, 1963: In his State of the Union address, President John Kennedy says the right to vote should not be denied to any citizen based on race or color.

January 31: Representative William McCulloch (R-Ohio), ranking Republican on the Judiciary Committee; Representative John Lindsay (R-New York); and other House Republicans introduce the first civil rights bill of the 88th Congress (1963–64).

February 28: President Kennedy sends his first civil rights bill—on voting and on extending the life of the Civil Rights Commission for four additional years—to Congress.

April 3: Massive civil rights demonstrations led by the Reverend Dr. Martin Luther King Jr. begin in Birmingham, Alabama.

April 4: Representative Emanuel Celler (D-New York), chairman of the House Judiciary Committee, introduces legislation on President Kennedy's voting and Civil Rights Commission proposals.

CHAPTER 3

CHAPTER 11

October 26: Rep. McCulloch works on a compromise bill. He reaches preliminary accord with Deputy AG Katzenbach on a number of outstanding issues after securing tentative backing from some Republicans.

October 27: Rep. McCulloch and Rep. Lindsay meet and resolve their differences on the bill. McCulloch arranges for Republican staffers Kimball and William Copenhaver to meet with Deputy AG Katzenbach and Burke Marshall, the assistant attorney general for civil rights.

CHAPTER 12

October 28: Joseph Alsop's column in the *New York Herald Tribune* and Anthony Lewis's *New York Times* article, in early-morning editions of the two newspapers, threaten bipartisan agreement.

CHAPTER 13

October 28: At 10:00 a.m., Deputy AG Katzenbach, Assistant AG Marshall, Copenhaver, and Kimball meet in room 410 of the Hotel Congressional and resolve differences between the McCulloch–Lindsay and Department of Justice–White House positions on the substitute bill. In an afternoon meeting at the White House, a group of northern Democrats agree to support the substitute bill.

CHAPTER 14

October 29: At 8:30 a.m., the House Judiciary Committee Republicans and the Republican leadership meet to discuss the substitute bill. House Minority Leader Charles Halleck (R-Indiana) and Rep. McCulloch visit the White House to inform President

Kennedy that eight of the 14 Republicans on the Judiciary Committee will support the substitute bill. At 10:30 a.m., the Judiciary Committee meeting begins. Rep. Moore's motion is defeated, and in a separate vote, the substitute bill is approved.

CHAPTER 17
From the Rules Committee to the House Floor,

January 9, 1964: Hearings on the civil rights bill begin in the
House Rules Committee and continue through January 29.

January 30: The Rules Committee clears the bill for House debate.

January 31: Debate begins in the House of Representatives.

February 10: The debate in the House concludes with passage of
the civil rights bill.

June 19: The Senate passes the civil rights bill.

July 2: President Johnson signs the 1964 Civil Rights Act.

Key Players

House of Representatives: Republicans

NAME	STATE	ROLE
ARENDS, LES	Illinois	Republican Whip
BROMWELL, JAMES	Iowa	Judiciary Committee member
BROWN, CLARENCE	Ohio	Senior Republican on the Rules Committee
BYRNES, JOHN	Wisconsin	
CAHILL, WILLIAM	New Jersey	Judiciary Committee member
CRAMER, WILLIAM	Florida	Judiciary Committee member; Subcommittee No. 5 member
CURTIS, THOMAS	Missouri	
DEROUNIAN, STEVEN	New York	
FORD, GERALD	Michigan	
GRIFFIN, ROBERT	Michigan	Education and Labor Committee member
GROSS, H.R.	Iowa	
HALL, DURWARD "DOC"	Missouri	
HALLECK, CHARLES	Indiana	House Minority Leader
KING, CARLTON	New York	Judiciary Committee member
LAIRD, MELVIN	Wisconsin	
LINDSAY, JOHN	New York	Judiciary Committee member
MACGREGOR, CLARK	Minnesota	Judiciary Committee member
MAILLIARD, WILLIAM	California	
MARTIN, PATRICK MINOR	California	Judiciary Committee member
MATHIAS, CHARLES	Maryland	Judiciary Committee member
MCCULLOCH, WILLIAM	Ohio	Ranking Republican Judiciary Committee member; Subcommittee No. 5 member

(continued)

MEADER, GEORGE	Michigan	Judiciary Committee member; Subcommittee No. 5 member
MILLER, WILLIAM	New York	Judiciary Committee member; Subcommittee No. 5 member; Republican National Committee chairman
MOORE, ARCH	West Virginia	Judiciary Committee member
POFF, RICHARD	Virginia	Judiciary Committee member
RHODES, JOHN	Arizona	
SCHWENGEL, FRED	Iowa	
SHRIVER, GARNER	Kansas	Judiciary Committee member
SMITH, H. ALLEN	California	Rules Committee member
SPRINGER, WILLIAM	Illinois	
ST. GEORGE, KATHARINE	New York	Rules Committee member
TEAGUE, CHARLES	California	
WILSON, BOB	California	

House of Representatives: Democrats

NAME	STATE	ROLE
ALBERT, CARL	Oklahoma	House Majority Leader
ASHMORE, ROBERT	South Carolina	Judiciary Committee member
BOGGS, HALE	Louisiana	Democratic Whip
BOLLING, RICHARD	Missouri	Rules Committee member; Leader of Democratic Study Group (DSG) Task Force on Civil Rights
BROOKS, JACK	Texas	Judiciary Committee member; Subcommittee No. 5 member
CELLER, EMANUEL	New York	Judiciary Committee chairman; Subcommittee No. 5 chairman
CORMAN, JAMES	California	Judiciary Committee member
DONAHUE, HAROLD	Massachusetts	Judiciary Committee member; Subcommittee No. 5 member
EDWARDS, DON	California	Judiciary Committee member
ELLIOT, CARL	Alabama	Rules Committee member
FORRESTER, ELIJAH "TIC"	Georgia	Judiciary Committee member
FRASER, DONALD	Minnesota	
GILBERT, JACOB	New York	Judiciary Committee member
GILL, THOMAS	Hawaii	
HARRIS, OREN	Arkansas	
KASTENMEIER, ROBERT	Wisconsin	Judiciary Committee member; Subcommittee No. 5 member
KEOGH, EUGENE	New York	Ways and Means Committee member; Committee of the Whole chairman

(continued)

LIBONATI, RONALD	Illinois	Judiciary Committee member
MCCORMACK, JOHN	Massachusetts	Speaker
O'HARA, BARRATT	Illinois	
POWELL, ADAM CLAYTON	New York	Committee on Education and Labor chairman
RODINO, PETER	New Jersey	Judiciary Committee member; Subcommittee No. 5 member
ROGERS, BYRON	Colorado	Judiciary Committee member; Subcommittee No. 5 member
ROOSEVELT, JAMES	California	
RYAN, WILLIAM FITTS	New York	
SCOTT, RALPH	North Carolina	
SMITH, HOWARD	Virginia	Rules Committee chairman
THOMPSON, FRANK	New Jersey	
TOLL, HERMAN	Pennsylvania	Judiciary Committee member; Subcommittee No. 5 member
TUCK, WILLIAM	Virginia	Judiciary Committee member
VINSON, CARL	Georgia	House Armed Services Committee chairman
WALTER, FRANCES	Pennsylvania	Judiciary Committee member; House Un-American Activities Committee chairman
WILLIAMS, JOHN BELL	Mississippi	
WILLIS, EDWIN	Louisiana	Leader of the Judiciary Committee Southern Democrats

House of Representatives: Staff

COPENHAVER, WILLIAM	Minority counsel for the Judiciary Committee
DESCHLER, LEW	House of Representatives parliamentarian
DICK, BESS	Staff director
FOLEY, WILLIAM	Judiciary Committee counsel
FUCHS, HERB	Judiciary Committee counsel
ZELENKO, BENJAMIN	Judiciary Committee counsel

Journalists

ABERNATHY, BOB	NBC
ALSOP, JOSEPH	Syndicated columnist
AVERILL, JOHN	The Los Angeles Times
BARTLETT, CHARLES	Syndicated columnist
BECKLER, JOHN	Associated Press
BLAIR, ANN	Triangle Publications
DRUMMOND, ROSCOE	Syndicated columnist
EVANS, ROWLAND	Syndicated columnist with Robert Novak
FLEESON, DORIS	Syndicated columnist
GLASS, ANDREW	New York Herald Tribune
GREENFIELD, MEG	The Reporter
KEMPTON, MURRAY	New Republic
KENWORTHY, E.W. (NED)	The New York Times
KROCK, ARTHUR	Syndicated columnist
KUMPA, PETER	The Baltimore Sun
LAWRENCE, DAVID	Syndicated columnist
LEWIS, ANTHONY	The New York Times
LINDSAY, JOHN	Newsweek
LIPPMANN, WALTER	Syndicated columnist
LOFTUS, JOSEPH	The New York Times
LYONS, RICHARD	The Washington Post

(continued)

MACKIN, CATHERINE	Hearst Headline Service
MCGRORY, MARY	Syndicated columnist
MILLER, LOYE	Time magazine
NOVAK, ROBERT	Syndicated columnist with Rowland Evans
PEARSON, DREW	Syndicated columnist
RESTON, JAMES	Syndicated columnist
SAWISLAK, ARNOLD	United Press International
SEMPLE JR., ROBERT B.	The New York Times
SPIVACK, ROBERT G.	Syndicated columnist
SULLIVAN, JOSEPH	The Wall Street Journal
WALSH, ROBERT	The Washington Star
WHITE, WILLIAM	Syndicated columnist

Administration Officials during the presidencies of John F. Kennedy and Lyndon B. Johnson

KATZENBACH, NICHOLAS	Deputy Attorney General
KENNEDY, ROBERT	Attorney General
MARSHALL, BURKE	Assistant Attorney General for Civil Rights
O'BRIEN, LAWRENCE	Congressional Relations Chief for the White House

xx CRISIS AND COMPROMISE

Organization Officials

AGREE, GEORGE	National Committee for an Effective Congress
ARONSON, ARNOLD	Secretary of the Leadership Conference on Civil Rights
BIEMILLER, ANDREW	Chief lobbyist for the AFL-CIO
COHEN, DAVID	Americans for Democratic Action (ADA)
DUBROW, EVELYN	International Ladies Garment Workers Union (ILGWU)
HIGGS, BILL	Washington representative of Student Nonviolent Coordinating Committee (SNCC)
HILL, HERBERT	NAACP
HOFFA, JAMES	Teamsters head
KING JR., DR. MARTIN LUTHER	President of the Southern Christian Leadership Conference
MITCHELL JR., CLARENCE	Washington representative for the NAACP
MOSES, ROBERT	Student Nonviolent Coordinating Committee (SNCC)/Voter registration activist
PHILLIPS, BILL	Democratic Study Group (DSG)
POHLHAUS, FRANCIS	NAACP
RAUH JR., JOSEPH	Counsel to the Leadership Conference on Civil Rights; Americans for Democratic Action (ADA)
REUTHER, WALTER	United Auto Workers leader
ROTHMAN, STUART	Former general counsel to the National Labor Relations Board
WILKINS, ROY	Executive Secretary (Head) of NAACP
ZAGRI, SIDNEY	Chief lobbyist for the Teamsters

Introduction

In late October 1963, the quest for comprehensive bipartisan civil rights legislation in the US Congress was in serious trouble, bogged down in a quagmire of partisan and sectional wrangling in the Judiciary Committee of the House of Representatives. After months of hope, turmoil, legislative initiatives, and extended public hearings in the House, there was still no accord regarding the shape or intricate details of a bill to address inequality in voting rights; access to public accommodations, education, and employment; the non-discriminatory use of federal funds; and the future of the Civil Rights Commission, created in 1957 to help enforce civil rights laws.

It had been a year highlighted by demands for change: civil rights demonstrations and a massive police response in Birmingham, Alabama; weeks of testimony before the House Judiciary Committee; the June assassination of Medgar Evers, a National Association for the Advancement of Colored People (NAACP) leader, in Mississippi; a major address to the nation on the need for civil rights legislation by President John F. Kennedy; the epochal August 28

March on Washington for Jobs and Freedom, capped by the Reverend Dr. Martin Luther King Jr.'s extraordinary "I Have a Dream" speech at the Lincoln Memorial; and the mid-September bombing of the 16th Street Baptist Church in Birmingham, resulting in the death of four young Black girls. This was the backdrop for a tangled series of moves to find bipartisan congressional support for major civil rights legislation.

The tragedy of the Birmingham church bombing helped propel the legislation forward, leading the House Judiciary Committee's Subcommittee No. 5, whose jurisdiction included civil rights, to strengthen the pending civil rights bill and send it to the entire Judiciary Committee for a vote—a bill that many on the full committee felt would be too sweeping to win House and then Senate approval. Attorney General Robert Kennedy's mid-October testimony indicated he was in favor—if at times equivocally—of more moderate legislation, which prompted a surprise motion by Representative Arch Moore, Republican of West Virginia.

Formulated far from Washington, DC—in a hotel in Geneva, Switzerland, where Rep. Moore was attending a conference—his proposal sought to bypass the full Judiciary Committee and what he saw as stalled deliberations. Moore wished to report out the broader subcommittee bill without the moderate changes suggested by Attorney General Kennedy. This development produced an unlikely union between the bill's most ardent advocates, including national civil rights groups, and southern opponents of the legislation, who were confident they would be able to defeat or cripple the bill because it was so broad.

The Moore motion, introduced at the full Judiciary Committee session on October 22, 1963, was like a sword of Damocles hanging over the legislation. Could the Kennedy administration, which had made clear it wanted bipartisan support for civil rights legislation, work with the moderates on both sides of the aisle and defeat the Moore motion in the Judiciary Committee, and then reach a compromise that would win a majority for the legislation on the House floor? Or was there enough support among unlikely allies—civil rights proponents and southerners opposing those rights—to pass the Moore motion?

Over the next few days, from October 23 to 29, the battle lines hardened. As the fate of what would eventually emerge as the Civil Rights Act of 1964 hung in the balance, discussions were taking place to produce a measure that would not fully satisfy the civil rights groups but would have the backing of President Kennedy and a majority of the House Republicans and northern Democrats.

On October 27, a key development occurred when moderate-conservative Republican William M. McCulloch of Ohio and liberal Republican John V. Lindsay of New York, both influential members of the House Judiciary Committee, met in Representative McCulloch's office and resolved their differences on the bill, thus improving the chances that a majority of the other 12 Republican members of the committee would support a bipartisan compromise. McCulloch, with Representative Lindsay's backing, asked Deputy Attorney General Nicholas Katzenbach and Burke Marshall, chief of the Department of Justice Civil Rights Division, to sit down with House

Republican representatives to work out details of a compromise measure that the president could offer to northern Democrats for their approval.

A crucial meeting to hammer out a bipartisan agreement took place on the morning of Monday, October 28, in room 410 of the Hotel Congressional, just a block from the Capitol. Four people were present: Deputy Attorney General Katzenbach and Assistant Attorney General Marshall representing the Kennedy administration, William Copenhaver, minority counsel of the House Judiciary Committee, and me, representing the House Republicans. I was 24 years old and in charge of a new congressional support organization called the Republican Legislative Research Association (RLRA), created to provide staff assistance to Republican representatives in connection with the civil rights legislative effort.

In this position, I was the principal House Republican staff member for shaping strategy and working with the House Republicans on civil rights legislation. I came to this post after serving as legislative assistant to Rep. Lindsay, later mayor of New York City. I had also developed good personal relationships with House Republican congressmen and staff members including, notably, Minority Leader Charles A. Halleck of Indiana and Rep. McCulloch, the ranking Republican on the House Judiciary Committee.

McCulloch became my mentor and friend. I was frequently asked to sit in his office when he had meetings and telephone conversations about the legislation. At the direction of McCulloch, Lindsay, Halleck, and others, I met with such instrumental figures as Attorney General Kennedy; NAACP leaders Roy Wilkins and Clarence Mitchell Jr.; teamster chief James Hoffa; Student Nonviolent Coordinating Committee/SNCC voter registration hero Robert "Bob" Moses (not to be confused with New York City urban planner Robert Moses); Judiciary Committee Chairman Emanuel Celler and his staff; southern Democratic chieftains Howard Smith of Virginia, the Rules Committee chairman, and Edwin Willis of Louisiana, leader of the House Judiciary southern Democrats; Joseph Rauh Jr. of Americans for Democratic Action (ADA); and United Auto Workers leader Walter Reuther; as well as many church and labor officials, members of the United States Senate, and virtually every reporter and columnist writing about the legislation, including E. W. "Ned" Kenworthy and Anthony Lewis of the *New York Times*.

This book focuses chiefly on the events of that turbulent fall, from the Birmingham church bombing on September 15 to the compromise of late October, which preceded the passage of the civil rights legislation by the House of Representatives on February 10, 1964. In particular, it addresses the largely overlooked role of the House Republicans in the success of that legislation. Many readers will be surprised to learn that leading up to the Civil Rights Act of 1964, House Republicans had introduced more civil rights bills—and had introduced them earlier—than House Democrats did. The February 10 vote was 290–130; 78 percent of Republicans voted in favor of the measure, while only 59 percent of the Democrats supported it.

In 2014, to coincide with the 50th anniversary of the Civil Rights Act, two important books were published by distinguished journalists: Todd S. Purdum's *An Idea Whose Time Has Come: Two Presidents, Two Parties, and the Battle for the Civil Rights Act of 1964* (Henry Holt and Company) and Clay Risen's *The Bill of the Century: The Epic Battle for the Civil Rights Act* (Bloomsbury Press). While both books give a fair amount of attention to the proceedings in the House of Representatives, they devote much more space to the developments in the Senate and to the policies and participation of the Kennedy and Johnson administrations. John Stewart, legislative assistant to Senator Hubert Humphrey, Democrat of Minnesota, also wrote extensively about the progress of the civil rights bill in the US Senate; this material is included in *The Civil Rights Act of 1964: The Passage of the Law That Ended Racial Segregation*, edited by Robert D. Loevy (SUNY Press, 1997).

Prior to this, the most notable book about the role of Congress in shaping the landmark 1964 legislation was *The Longest Debate: A Legislative History of the 1964 Civil Rights Act* by the husband-and-wife team Charles and Barbara Whalen (Seven Locks Press, 1985). Charles was a member of Congress from Ohio from 1967 to 1979; Barbara was a newspaper columnist, advertising executive, and television continuity writer. Their book is informative and well-researched and devotes considerable attention to events in the House of Representatives and the role of the House Republicans. However, perhaps because neither of them was in Washington at the time of this remarkable legislative struggle, they omit or do not adequately explain some significant events regarding the story behind the House's version of the omnibus bill.

I was interviewed by Purdum, Risen, and the Whalens, and I am cited and quoted in their books. Yet my book is, to my knowledge, the first detailed account by an actual participant in the fraught journey and dramatic rescue of civil rights legislation in the House of Representatives. It is the story, not fully or always accurately reported, of how the vast majority of House Republicans put aside thoughts of political advantage and worked to enact bipartisan legislation despite the temptation to defeat the bill and embarrass the Democratic administration.

Representative Halleck, who later paid the political price for his support of civil rights, told me at the time that it was vital to describe that effort. He believed someone should chronicle how the House of Representatives dealt with that historical legislation during the last months of John F. Kennedy's presidency and the early days of Lyndon Johnson's administration. "Otherwise," he said, "no one is going to write—or believe—that the House Republicans had any positive role in the struggle for civil rights legislation." And he added one suggestion: "You should write it."

Drawing on the extensive files I maintained at that time, including a journal of my activity during the crucial deliberations, a record of the many phone calls I made and received, and copious notes on meetings I attended— in addition to newspaper clippings and transcripts of testimony and debates (many of which are listed in the

References section of this book)—I have finally made good on Representative Halleck's suggestion.

* * *

For those who have known me over the years as a musical theater historian and are mystified to see my name on a book about the Civil Rights Act of 1964, I should explain my involvement with that historic legislation.

During the summer of 1961, immediately after my graduation from Yale College as an American Studies major, I worked as an intern in Washington, DC, for Rep. Lindsay. At the end of the summer, I returned to Yale to serve as a teaching fellow in American history in conjunction with a Carnegie fellowship for the 1961–62 academic year. When I received a letter from Rep. Lindsay asking me to return to his office to serve as his legislative assistant, I eagerly accepted. Between May 1962 and the summer of 1963, I worked full time in this position, which allowed me to participate in discussions about many bills introduced in the House of Representatives—including civil rights legislation.

In the summer of 1963, as the civil rights legislative battle began to heat up, George Agree of the National Committee for an Effective Congress approached me on behalf of Alfred Landon, the Republican presidential candidate in 1936, and Charles Taft, a member of the distinguished Republican political family, with the unique opportunity to run the RLRA. This new job required that I reach out to and engage in dialogue with Republican members of the

House and their staff members, with the aim of mobilizing backing for the legislation. Funding for my work with the RLRA, as for Democrat legislative research staff support, came from two primary sources outside of government: Stephen Currier of the Taconic Foundation and the DeWitt Wallace family, who owned *Reader's Digest*. Meanwhile, I continued to serve as Rep. Lindsay's legislative assistant.

I was supposed to start Yale Law School in the fall of 1963, but many people involved in the civil rights effort urged me to stay in Washington to continue my work with the RLRA. Among those who persuaded the dean of Yale Law School to defer my enrollment were Roy Wilkins, head of the NAACP; Senator Hugh Scott, Republican of Pennsylvania; and Rep. McCulloch, who, in encouraging me not to leave DC, said, "This could be the most important matter we ever work on."

I eventually entered Yale Law School in 1964 and graduated in 1967, but after those heady, historically momentous days in Washington, I did not see a meaningful role for myself in government or politics. And I never practiced law.

As an undergraduate, I had written my senior paper on the American musical in the 1920s. In my last year of law school, my undergraduate advisor was asked to organize the papers that songwriter Cole Porter had left to Yale, his alma mater. Too ill to take on the task, he recruited me for that assignment, which turned out to be the beginning of a lifelong career. My longstanding interest in American musical theater proved stronger than the appeal of the law, and I became a recognized scholar, author, and editor in that field. But with unexpected free time during the COVID-19 pandemic, I revisited the book I had started decades earlier about the Civil Rights Act. I soon realized that in today's polarized environment, the book's message about the importance of bipartisanship is still relevant.

Some of the notes I kept in the fall of 1963, in the midst of the fight for civil rights legislation, appear almost verbatim in this book. As I reread my impressions from more than half a century ago, I am reminded of how passionately committed I was to helping the liberal-moderate wing of the Republican Party ensure that the House would pass the Civil Rights Act. I am also deeply saddened by this reminder that since my time in Washington, liberal-moderate Republicans have become not just an endangered species, but virtually extinct. I wonder if younger Americans now are aware that they ever existed.

As a participant in the legislative drama surrounding the bill, I was a witness to only a portion of the vast battlefield through which it progressed. Nonetheless, one of my hopes is that this book will give readers a more complete view of the Republican Party's constructive but largely unheralded role in the civil rights fight. The House Republicans' willingness to compromise proved crucial in fashioning a bipartisan agreement. Yet that compromise, reached during the final days of President Kennedy's life, would be much more difficult (if not impossible) to achieve amid the rancorous climate in Washington today. In fact, partisan wrangling has intensified to such an extent that this kind of agreement would seem entirely out of reach.

*   *   *

When I look back on the struggle to pass a civil rights bill in the fall of 1963, I have fond memories of my colleagues at the decisive Hotel Congressional meeting on October 28, and of our discussion that helped shape the compromise that cleared the House Judiciary Committee the following day. Sadly, all three men—shrewd, tough, persistent Deputy AG Katzenbach; scholarly, mild-mannered, thoughtful Assistant AG Marshall; and Copenhaver, a fine lawyer and my friend and collaborator—have departed this life. I miss them and honor the memory of these great men. I hope they would not find too much to question in my account of our joint activities.

Finally, I owe a special debt to the two House Republican congressmen who had the greatest impact on the 1964 Civil Rights Act—John Lindsay and William McCulloch.

Lindsay, who represented the so-called Silk Stocking District (because it included the Upper East Side of Manhattan), was born in New York City on November 24, 1921. He was a graduate of St. Paul's School in Concord, New Hampshire; Yale College; and Yale Law School. During World War II, as a Navy officer on a destroyer, he participated in landings on Sicily and in the Pacific. He later practiced law at the New York firm of Webster and Sheffield and served as an executive assistant to US Attorney General Herbert Brownell Jr. before his 1958 election to the 86th Congress and his subsequent reelection to the 87th, 88th, and 89th Congresses. He then served two terms as mayor of New York City, from 1966 to 1973, switching his allegiance to the Democratic Party in 1971. He died in 2000.

McCulloch was born on a family farm near Holmesville, Ohio, on November 24, 1901, exactly 20 years before Lindsay—although I never heard the two men speak about the coincidence. Holmesville is five miles from Millersburg, county seat of Wooster, and 75 miles south of Cleveland. After high school, McCulloch attended the College of Wooster in Wooster, Ohio, and then Ohio State University School of Law, where he received his bachelor of law in June 1925. After graduation he returned to Holmesville to teach high school for one year before moving to Jacksonville, Florida, where he began the practice of law. While working in Jacksonville, at the height of the Florida land boom, he encountered racial prejudice, which profoundly influenced his passion for equal rights and his future as a champion of racial equality.

Through the family of his wife, Mabel, whom he married in 1927, McCulloch found a position as a lawyer in Piqua, Ohio. He served six terms in the Ohio House of Representatives, was minority leader from 1936 to 1939, and was Speaker for three terms. After serving in World War II, he was elected to the 80th Congress in 1947 from a west-central Ohio congressional district that included Piqua; the cities of Lima, Troy, Sidney, Greenville (home of the celebrated Darke County Fair), and Wapakoneta (birthplace of astronaut Neil Armstrong); and much rich farm country. McCulloch was reelected to each succeeding Congress until his retirement in 1972. He died in 1980.

Though very different from one another in many ways, these two men had tremendous respect for each other and worked together tirelessly as leaders in the fight for civil rights legislation in 1963–64.

With the emergence of conservative Senator Barry Goldwater in 1964 as the Republican presidential candidate, the character of the Republican Party changed rapidly. Although I remained registered as a Republican, I invariably voted for Democratic candidates for local and national office.

I finally reached the breaking point in 2016 when Donald Trump became the Republican Party nominee for president. While having dinner with my family at a restaurant in Brooklyn, on the spur of the moment I used an iPhone to change my party registration to Democrat. I still honor Rep. Lindsay, Rep. McCulloch, and the other Republicans I worked with in the early 1960s and their achievements in the civil rights arena. It is obvious, however, that more than a half-century later, the fight for equal rights and social justice is not over.

Robert Kimball
New York City
April 2021

CHAPTER 1

Memories of Capitol Hill
1962

After all these years, I can still recall some of the sounds on the Hill—the clatter of the office machines, the hubbub as members made their way from their Capitol offices to the House Chamber. Above all, I hear the voice of reading clerk Joe Bartlett as he intoned the members' names for a quorum call or called the roll for the yeas and nays—"Abbott, Abernathy, Adair, Addabbo . . ."—which gave members at least 15 minutes to walk from the Longworth or Cannon office buildings to the House floor. Of course, those were long-ago times when there was no electronic voting and tight security was not required.

If you arrived on Capitol Hill early enough in the morning—say, before 7:00 a.m.—you could head for the House Office Building cafeteria and, if you were lucky, have breakfast with "the Admiral": Democrat Representative Carl Vinson of Milledgeville, Georgia, venerable chairman of the House Armed Services Committee. Born in 1883, Vinson had served in the House of Representatives since 1914. Whenever he was in town, the Admiral led the House cafeteria breakfast line. With the death of Speaker Sam Rayburn in 1961, during the 87th Congress, Vinson had become the senior member of the House.

As my morning progressed, there was the mail—always the mail—plus speeches to draft, press releases to write, and congressional testimony to prepare. There were also visits by constituents hoping for a glimpse of (or a word with) my boss, Congressman John Lindsay, and the procession of lobbyists for or against one cause or another. A frequent highlight of our day was the arrival of staff members from the office of San Francisco Republican William Mailliard, who would come to borrow our Robotype machine. The Mailliard staffers all looked as if they had been flight attendants or beauty contest participants, and in those less politically correct times, they were known in Representative Lindsay's office as "Mailliard's babes."

Often there were meetings with interest groups who were purportedly from your congressional district, although it sometimes turned out that not a single person present in the room was actually from your district. Walking through the halls was amusing because anyone could say hello to members of Congress knowing they would invariably respond, as they had no way of determining whether or not the person was a constituent.

Sometimes, humorous mistakes were made. New York Republican Senator Kenneth Keating's office once asked Rep. Lindsay's office to insert in the Congressional Record a speech the senator had delivered at a Yeshiva University graduation. However, his staff had mistakenly attached an introduction Sen. Keating had delivered to a Catholic school. Fortunately, we spotted the error in time after we discovered another Keating speech that coupled the Catholic school speech with the Yeshiva introduction.

I remember one time we almost made an error by sending out letters for people who had just been inducted into the armed forces, welcoming them as new citizens instead. Some of the humor, however, was intentional. At lunchtime in the cafeteria, you could amuse your friends by having them paged over the loudspeaker. If you wanted to enhance your own self-importance, you could have yourself paged.

An interesting luncheon alternative was the very fine restaurant in the Teamsters building, where I once had a memorable meal with Sidney Zagri, chief lobbyist for the Teamsters, and his boss, the forceful, charismatic Jimmy Hoffa. When he spoke, Hoffa would push his fingers against my chest to emphasize what he was saying. I knew Zagri well because, at the request of Senator Wayne Morse, Democrat of Oregon, I did some research for the Teamsters and helped them prepare their testimony on civil rights legislation. During my years on the Hill, I found that the most impressive and effective lobbyists for or against legislation were the Teamster wives. The Teamsters also hosted the Washington Film Society, where one could see a number of classic foreign films.

Back in the office after lunch, there was more mail, of course—sending form letters to supporters and opponents of a member's position on a particular matter ("Thank you for the benefit of your views") and putting "buck slips" on items that needed a government agency response or research assistance from the Legislative Reference Service of the Library of Congress. Then there were statements and speeches to write for, say, Soviet-occupied Estonia, Latvia, and Lithuania during Captive Nations Week, or anniversary celebrations for certain interest groups.

On occasion I went to gatherings to promote Rep. Lindsay's legislative initiatives. One afternoon, I was sent to represent Lindsay at a meeting of senior citizens, which had been coordinated by Democratic Congressman Eugene Keogh of Brooklyn to discuss Medicare legislation. I arrived at the Caucus Room of the Old (Cannon) House Office Building with an armful of literature on Lindsay's Medicare bill, only to discover that no one was present but Representative Keogh, who was standing at the front of the room, gazing at his watch.

At first, Rep. Keogh—that paragon of sartorial splendor; that modern-day Jimmy Walker in charm and brassiness; that model of courtesy, dignity, and ready wit in his dealings with others—said nothing to me, merely responding to my greeting. Then, noting the stack of materials in my arms, he began to laugh. "What fancy literature!" he exclaimed. "Why, it puts one to shame to see such fine glossy stuff."

A group of his colleagues entered the room. Keogh immediately introduced me to them as "Mr. Lindsay's boy, who has brought over a great pile of Mr. Lindsay's lovely literature, which tells all about how Mr. Lindsay is the author of Medicare."

I was too embarrassed to say anything, knowing I would be verbally demolished if I did. I also knew that neither Rep. Keogh nor any of his Democratic colleagues, who were having a good laugh at my expense, went in for glossy brochures. When it became apparent that the senior citizens were not going to show up that afternoon, I gathered up the literature and returned to our office, a fairly dejected stand-in. I knew that if Rep. Lindsay had been there, he would have handled it much more gracefully.

Fortunately for me, the incident led to brighter things. A few days later, as I was trudging down a corridor of the House Office Building, I heard a voice hailing me: "Good day, Mr. Kimball."

I wheeled around, and there was Rep. Keogh, his hand outstretched, asking in that wonderful Brooklyn brogue whether I had recovered from the harsh treatment he had accorded me at our previous meeting. I stammered out a respectful reply.

He then said if I should ever need his assistance on any matters within the domain of the Ways and Means Committee, on which he was a senior member, or anything else—despite the fact that Rep. Lindsay was "a bogus Republican"—I should come to his office. If he wasn't there, his assistant Agnes Mathison would be glad to help me. Before I could thank him, he had ducked into the Ways and Means Committee room.

I was to take advantage of Rep. Keogh's kind offer on many occasions. When our office was looking to overhaul the tax structure or modify the Social Security Act, and the path had been trodden previously by Keogh, we put in the Keogh version and were always pleased to co-sponsor the proposal with the distinguished gentleman from Brooklyn. For we knew that if Ways and Means was going to report out a bill on a subject that had been introduced by many members already, there was a fairly good chance the committee would pick the Keogh bill—and almost no chance it would pick the Lindsay bill. So when "the Keogh–Lindsay bill" was reported from the Ways and Means Committee, we were always pleased.

Rep. Keogh went on to achieve renown as the author of the Keogh plans, which would give individuals a chance to save money on their taxes. Interestingly, neither Keogh nor his redoubtable assistant Agnes Mathison, whom I came to know and admire, wrote their biography for the congressional and staff directories. Few others on the Hill were as modest.

On one occasion, in the summer of 1961, I even met Speaker Sam Rayburn, Democrat of Texas, just months before he died. It was in the men's room in the Capitol Building. We were standing next to each other at the urinals when he patted my arm and said, "How are you, son?"

One memorable example of a celebratory event was the 50th anniversary of Actors' Equity—the union for Broadway and other performers. The union had little difficulty persuading the US Senate to proclaim an Actors' Equity Week, but things did not go so smoothly in the

House. It seems that the chairman of the Subcommittee on Holidays held up consideration of the bill, saying he wouldn't advance it unless and until he got "some New York f---ing." I soon realized his intentions: Actors' Equity would have to supply this congressman with a coterie of unemployed actresses for an entertaining weekend in New York. Apparently, that's what they did—and the bill passed. I can still remember Rep. Lindsay's wife, Mary, laughing at our haplessness in summoning enough courage to ask the union to arrange for the congressman's Gotham pleasures.

It wasn't always as crazy as this.

As the typical day ground to a halt, you had to remember to call most House offices before 4:45 p.m., as many staff members already were headed for the parking lots to begin the ride home. There were plenty of choices for dinner, especially if you were planning to head back to the office afterwards—including Duke Zeibert's; The Monocle, near the Senate; or Wearley's, near the Dodge House, which was adorned with framed and mounted photographs of members of Congress and other notables.

Mike Palm's, on Pennsylvania Avenue, was a frequent dinner stop. I remember sitting there one night with Representative Ralph Scott, Democrat of North Carolina, who told me almost tearfully that he never should have run for Congress (he had been elected first in 1956) and that he really should quit and "go home." On another occasion, I was surprised to see a most unlikely duo—Representative Charles Halleck, Republican minority leader from Indiana, sitting at a table with Representative William Fitts

Ryan, a liberal Democrat from New York City. To this day, I wonder what they talked about.

One member whom I admired, but who struck me as rather solitary, was House Majority Leader Carl Albert, Democrat of Oklahoma. I often saw Representative Albert walking slowly near the Capitol with his head bowed in contemplation. He sometimes had dinner alone in the dining room at the Hotel Congressional. A fixture at night in the Congressional dining room was 80-year-old House Democrat Barratt O'Hara of Chicago, who long ago had been an explorer and sports reporter. He was always with his administrative assistant, Marie Crowe. Together they prepared digests of all the recently enacted public laws and sent them to many of O'Hara's Chicago constituents—an unusual public service.

It was at a dinner at the Hotel Congressional in early September 1962 that Representative Thomas Curtis, Republican of Missouri, devised the strategy that helped defeat the Industrial Security Bill. This marked the first time that the House Un-American Activities Committee (or HUAC), chaired by Representative Francis Walter of Pennsylvania, had been rebuffed in a legislative battle on the House floor. Members were reluctant to defy Rep. Walter because he had control over private immigration bills, parking spots, and many Capitol patronage jobs such as pages and elevator operators. So Rep. Curtis persuaded two Republicans—Lindsay, and one other—and three Democrats to sign a joint letter urging defeat of the controversial legislation on procedural grounds, saying that a measure of such importance should not be pushed through Congress either under unanimous consent or by suspension of the rules requiring passage with a two-thirds majority and only limited debate. The bill would not have been voted down without bipartisan support.

While the House office buildings normally were quiet on weekends, activity often continued at the Longworth office of Representative William McCulloch, Republican of Ohio, who collected the daily Congressional Records from the mail room and anywhere else he could find them, stamped them COMPLIMENTS OF THE FOURTH DISTRICT OF OHIO, and sent them to selected constituents. You could often see him at work in his shirtsleeves, stamping the Congressional Records himself.

For me, a special feature of Rep. McCulloch's office was the framed quotation from 18th-century statesman Edmund Burke's speech to the electors of Bristol, England, about the duty of an elected representative to his constituents.

McCulloch was of Scottish descent and proud of the careful way he spent money ("I am a generous man except where money is concerned"). One year when he was running for reelection, instead of hiring an actor to intone radio campaign ads for him, he saved money by reading the ads himself. Farmers in his district were often amused to hear, in the midst of radio reports of the early-morning egg prices, Congressman McCulloch extolling his own virtues (à la ice cream king Tom Carvel) with the music of the "Battle Hymn of the Republic" playing in the background.

It was at a late dinner in mid-September 1962 that Rep. Curtis of Missouri expressed to me his hope that at the opening of the 88th Congress in January 1963, the Republicans on the House Judiciary Committee would introduce a comprehensive civil rights bill. According to Rep. Curtis, introduction of the bill should be followed by a major speech-making and public relations campaign to persuade the Kennedy administration to join in pushing for the prompt enactment of civil rights legislation that, at a bare minimum, would carry out the civil rights plank of the 1960 Republican and Democratic platforms.

Curtis envisioned the civil rights effort as part of a sweeping Republican legislative offensive that would have experts on each House committee launch major programs in every area where Republicans were convinced that the national interest required federal legislation. He hoped that Rep. Lindsay of New York, Rep. McCulloch of Ohio, Representative Clark MacGregor of Minnesota, Representative Charles Mathias of Maryland, and others on the Judiciary Committee would jointly plan and co-sponsor the civil rights legislation. He pursued his suggestion by meeting with Reps. Lindsay and MacGregor in late September and with Lindsay alone after the 1962 congressional elections. Although he would play only a peripheral role in the drama of the 1963–64 civil rights battle, it was the conservative Curtis—one of the most able and enterprising members of the House—who helped spark the Republicans' civil rights initiative.

Many events had profoundly shaped attitudes on civil rights in America during the preceding decade. In 1954, the epochal US Supreme Court decision in *Brown v. Board of Education of Topeka* abolished segregation in

US public schools. Less than a year later, teenager Claudette Colvin was arrested in Montgomery, Alabama, for refusing to give up her seat on a city bus, which helped inspire Rosa Parks to do the same and led to the subsequent bus boycott.

In early 1956, after the Supreme Court upheld a lower court decision, the University of Alabama admitted Autherine Lucy as its first Black student. Her tenure there was brief, ending when a mob attacked her, and the university denied her permission to continue.

In the summer of 1957, Congress passed the first civil rights act of the century. Among its provisions was the creation of a Civil Rights Commission. That September, there was a major controversy over school desegregation in Arkansas. When the state's governor, Orval Faubus, employed National Guardsmen to prevent nine Black students from entering previously all-white Central High School in Little Rock, President Dwight Eisenhower sent federal troops to Little Rock to enforce desegregation.

A new form of protest began in early 1960 with sit-ins in Greensboro, North Carolina. Four Black college students declined to leave a Woolworth's lunch counter when they were denied service. Later that year, Congress passed the 1960 Civil Rights Act, which strengthened some of the voting provisions of the 1957 law.

In May 1961, Freedom Riders began to challenge segregationist obstacles to interstate travel by organizing interracial bus trips to locations in the South. Many riders were assaulted and others arrested for trying to use segregated washrooms in southern bus terminals.

In 1962, focus shifted to the University of Mississippi in Oxford, when riots erupted over the admission of Black student James Meredith. And there was chaos in Alabama in June 1963, when Governor George C. Wallace tried to block the admission of two Black students, Vivian Malone and James Hood, to the University of Alabama in Tuscaloosa. Gov. Wallace gave up when President Kennedy federalized the Alabama National Guard, and on June 11, the students were able to register. By then, the president had already begun to address the need for civil rights legislation.

CHAPTER 2

Tumult and Response
January 14–August 2, 1963

In his State of the Union address on January 14, 1963, President John F. Kennedy said, "The most precious and powerful right in the world, the right to vote in a free American election, must not be denied to any citizen on grounds of . . . race or color." But it was only a speech; it did not commit the Kennedy administration to press for the enactment of civil rights legislation during the 88th Congress.

In 1963–64, Democrats held the majority in the House (and the Senate), but it was 42 House Republicans—led by Rep. William McCulloch of Ohio, ranking minority member of the House Judiciary Committee, and Rep. John Lindsay of New York, with the tacit support of Minority Leader Charles Halleck of Indiana—who introduced, on

January 31, the first major civil rights bill of the 88th Congress. Originally drafted in December 1962 by Lindsay after his discussions with Rep. Tom Curtis of Missouri, the bill would have (1) made the Civil Rights Commission permanent and empowered it to investigate election fraud; (2) established a Federal Commission for Equality of Opportunity in federal contracts; (3) authorized the US attorney general to initiate lawsuits on behalf of citizens denied admission to segregated schools; (4) offered federal technical assistance to help states desegregate their schools; and (5) provided a rebuttable presumption—meaning that presumption could be challenged—of literacy for voting purposes in federal elections if an individual had completed six grades in school.

In preparing the legislation, Rep. Lindsay had received assistance from Clarence Mitchell Jr., Francis Pohlhaus, and Herbert Hill, all of the NAACP. The bill went through five drafts and was considered at length in at least a dozen meetings of the Republicans on the Judiciary Committee. Rep. McCulloch chaired the meetings, attended at one time or another by all 14 Republican members of the committee, including Representative Richard Poff of Virginia and Representative William Cramer of Florida. All 14 men contributed to the final product, which was introduced in the House by 10 of the committee's Republican members, including the party's national committee chairman, William Miller of New York.

A month later, on February 28, President Kennedy sent his first civil rights bill to Congress. He called for legislation to (1) authorize the appointment of temporary voting referees to register Black citizens in counties where suits were filed and less than 15 percent of the voting-age population was registered; (2) expedite the handling of voting rights suits in the federal courts; (3) make a sixth-grade education presumptive of literacy; (4) provide federal financial and technical assistance to school districts in the process of desegregating; and (5) extend the life of the Civil Rights Commission for four additional years, and authorize it to serve as a national clearinghouse for civil rights information.

Legislation carrying out the voting and Civil Rights Commission proposals of President Kennedy's bill was introduced on April 4 by Representative Emanuel "Manny" Celler, Democrat of New York, chairman of the House Judiciary Committee. The education provisions were not ready until April 23, when they were introduced by Representative James Roosevelt, a Democrat from California.

Meanwhile, on April 3, massive civil rights demonstrations began down in Birmingham, Alabama, led by the Reverend Dr. Martin Luther King Jr., president of the Southern Christian Leadership Conference. Fire hoses and police dogs met many thousands of demonstrators, including schoolchildren staging protest marches during early May. Scores of people were arrested for "parading without a permit." Images and descriptions of the action roused the nation to a new awareness of the difficult plight of Blacks in America and intensified efforts to guarantee full political and economic rights to the Black population.

The House Judiciary Committee held 22 days of hearings between May 8 and August 2 on all proposals for civil rights legislation put forth by Democrats and Republicans alike. Thirty-seven House Democrats from nine states introduced 83 bills, while 49 House Republicans from 20 states introduced 87 bills.

Representatives of interested groups testified before the Judiciary Committee, as did 14 House Democrats (nine northern and five southern) and 11 House Republicans. Although many groups were represented, few leading civil rights scholars and lawyers were urged to appear or specifically requested to testify. What could have been a searching inquiry into the nature of the American experience, and of the experience of the Black population in particular, ended up being a fairly routine, if somewhat more elaborate than usual, set of committee hearings.

On June 3, in the midst of the hearings, Rep. Lindsay, Rep. MacGregor of Minnesota, and more than 30 House Republicans introduced a bill supplementing the measures they had proposed back in January. This second House Republican bill invoked the 14th Amendment to outlaw segregation in stores, theaters, restaurants, and other public accommodations. The bill also included a version of the Title III provision—the word "title" referring to a large portion of a bill—dropped from the 1957 Civil Rights Act, authorizing the attorney general to institute legal proceedings against officials who deprived persons of their right to equal protection of the laws because of race, creed, or national origin. This bill was introduced without the support of Reps. McCulloch and Halleck.

On June 4, Reps. Lindsay and MacGregor took a two-hour special order to explain their bill on the House floor. I remember sitting in the gallery as their presentation was interrupted and delayed well into the night, as southern Democrats, led by Representative John Bell Williams of Mississippi, demanded repeated quorum calls—a tactic intended to harass the Republicans.

On June 11, President Kennedy delivered a major address to the nation about civil rights, becoming the first American president since Lincoln to make a total public commitment to the struggle for equal rights. The president followed up his address with a series of meetings with congressional leaders of both parties and leading Americans in many fields of endeavor, in an effort to secure broad nationwide support for civil rights legislation.

Eight days later, President Kennedy sent Congress a far-reaching civil rights bill that embraced the administration's February proposals as well as provisions to (1) secure equal access to places of public accommodation such as hotels, motels, restaurants, and stores, with provision for the attorney general to institute civil injunctive suits to bring about compliance; (2) give the federal government discretionary power to withhold any kind of federal financial assistance to any federal program when there was a finding of racial discrimination; (3) establish a federal Community Relations Service to cope with race-related problems at the local level; and (4) provide statutory authority for the President's Commission on Equal Employment Opportunity on government contracts. In the Judiciary Committee, Chairman Celler introduced the administration measure (H.R. 7152) on June 20.

A major clash occurred on June 26 between the House Judiciary Republicans and the Kennedy administration when Attorney General Robert Kennedy admitted, under aggressive questioning by Rep. Lindsay, that he had not read the civil rights bills submitted by the House Republicans. This touched off a lively skirmish in the committee and caused some Republicans to question the good faith of the administration's assertions that it wanted bipartisan cooperation on civil rights. The attorney general's testimony kicked off a parade of administration officials before the committee, including Labor Secretary Willard Wirtz; Health, Education, and Welfare Secretary Anthony Celebrezze; and a host of others.

A month later, the House Committee on Education and Labor reported a bill (H.R. 405) establishing a Federal Employment Practices Commission (FEPC) with power to prevent and eliminate discrimination by employers, unions, or the federal government. The commission was given authority to enforce its own decisions. Committee Chairman Adam Clayton Powell, Democrat of New York, immediately threatened to bring the bill to the floor of the House by the Calendar Wednesday procedure. Using this device, a committee chairman could expedite legislation reported by his committee without clearance by the House Rules Committee. Chairman Powell issued his threat primarily to force the Judiciary Committee to incorporate an FEPC into the omnibus civil rights bill.

A full-scale FEPC had not been included in either the

administration's bill or the two Republican measures of January 31 and June 3. In order to forestall the chaos and possible defeat of the FEPC bill under the Calendar Wednesday procedure, however, Rep. Celler and the House Democratic leadership privately agreed to Powell's demand.

On July 23, Representative Robert Kastenmeier, a liberal Democrat from Wisconsin, introduced perhaps the strongest, most comprehensive civil rights bill ever proposed in the US Congress. Incorporating many features from both the Kennedy administration and House Republican measures, Rep. Kastenmeier's bill went further in a number of respects. Where both the administration and Republican bills had limited their coverage to federal elections, Kastenmeier's title on voting embraced all elections. Kastenmeier's bill also strengthened both the scope and the strength of the enforcement provisions of previous voting legislation.

Rep. Kastenmeier's title on accommodations (referring to any place or business establishment that provides lodging, entertainment, dining, retail, or services to the public)—Title II—included all businesses licensed by the state and employed the 14th Amendment to the full extent of its reach. Kastenmeier also offered a broader Title III—on the power of the attorney general to initiate or intervene in litigation involving denial of equal protection of laws—than the comparable provision in the June Republican bill as well as a compulsory school plans provision. The Wisconsin Democrat's bill also called for a full-scale FEPC and anti-lynching provisions intended to further protect individuals from mob violence and police brutality motivated by racism.

Finally, Rep. Kastenmeier's bill expanded the removal sections of the United States Code (28 USC 1443) to make it easier to remove a case to a US district court whenever it appeared that strict impartiality was not possible in the state court. If removal was refused by the federal court, there was a right to appeal such removal to a higher federal court. The Student Nonviolent Coordinating Committee (SNCC) and the Washington Human Rights Project had assisted Kastenmeier in the preparation of his expansive bill.

By the time the House Judiciary Committee hearings on civil rights legislation came to an end on August 2, the committee had received voluminous testimony from a great many witnesses. It decided to focus its attention on four bills: H.R. 3139, introduced by McCulloch and other House Republicans in January; H.R. 6720, introduced by Lindsay and other House Republicans in June; H.R. 7152, the Kennedy administration bill, introduced by Celler and other House Democrats; and H.R. 7702, introduced by Kastenmeier.

CHAPTER 3

The Great March and the Birmingham Church Bombing
August 14–September 15, 1963

Now that the House Judiciary Committee had its four primary bills to consider, the first move belonged to the committee chair, Representative Celler. A veteran of 41 years in the House of Representatives, the Brooklyn Democrat was one of its sharpest practitioners of legislative politics. His marvelous wit, colorful turn of phrase, geniality, and shrewd understanding of the congressional process made him a general favorite among his colleagues. Prior to this new challenge, it had been his proud responsibility—as chairman of the Judiciary for every Democratic-controlled

Congress since 1949—to shepherd through the House the first, although limited, civil rights legislation since the Reconstruction era following the Civil War: the Civil Rights Acts of 1957 and 1960.

Over the years, Rep. Celler had developed a certain approach to handling civil rights measures, a strategy that brought credit to the northern wing of his own party and caused consternation among the Republicans. As chairman of the Judiciary Committee, it was his prerogative to refer all civil rights measures to Subcommittee No. 5, which he also chaired and which he had made a northern Democratic stronghold.

In the 88th Congress, the 11-person subcommittee was composed of seven Democrats and four Republicans. This gave the Democrats a somewhat more favorable ratio than their 21–14 majority in the full committee, or their 258–177 majority in the entire House of Representatives. It was no accident that six of the seven subcommittee Democrats (Chairman Celler of Brooklyn, New York; Peter Rodino of Newark, New Jersey; Byron Rogers of Denver, Colorado; Harold Donahue of Worcester, Massachusetts; Herman Toll of Philadelphia, Pennsylvania; and Robert Kastenmeier of Madison, Wisconsin)—a clear majority of the 11-man panel—hailed from northern and, with the exception of Rep. Kastenmeier, heavily urban areas. Jack Brooks of Beaumont, Texas, the seventh Democrat, was a moderate on racial matters. Therefore, among the Democratic members of Subcommittee No. 5, there were no all-out opponents of civil rights legislation—and Celler preferred it that way.

Of crucial significance to Chairman Celler, and to the early destiny of the civil rights bill, was the fact that the enclave of northern Democratic supremacy in the subcommittee was mirrored neither in the full committee nor in the House itself. Pro–civil rights Democrats comprised only 14 of the Judiciary Committee's 35 members and only 155 of the 435-member House. The more favorable ratio on Subcommittee No. 5, however, gave Celler and his cohorts the power to shape civil rights legislation in the fashion they desired.

Nevertheless, the group also knew any bill they reported out of committee would surely be altered along the tortuous paths of the legislative journey. For this eventuality, Celler planned a simple yet potentially brilliant strategy. He and his pro–civil rights, northern, urban Democratic allies would draft a strong bill in subcommittee that would satisfy most of the legislative demands of civil rights enthusiasts, spearheaded by the Leadership Conference on Civil Rights, an umbrella organization founded in 1950 of groups with a shared commitment to social justice. Celler would then report the bill to the full committee, heralded by salvos of praise from the civil rights groups, but with the expectation that Republicans and southern Democrats on the larger panel would modify the bill into a measure that could pass the House.

The advantages of this strategy to the Democratic Party were enticing. The northern Democrats, after receiving hosannas for having written the strongest possible bill, could blame the Republican–southern Democratic coalition for any subsequent weakening of the measure. The southerners could report happily to their constituents their success in trimming the rough edges off a stronger bill. And Republicans could be thrust once again into their customary role as opponents of progress. The success of Celler's strategy depended on one essential ingredient: a willingness among Republicans to support southern efforts to modify the strong subcommittee proposal. Since Republicans had complied readily in the past, there was every reason to anticipate that they would be equally obliging in this present civil rights struggle.

Celler was betting on more of the same behavior from Republicans as had occurred when the previous two civil rights bills passed Congress. During the effort that culminated in the 1957 Civil Rights Act, House Republicans on the Judiciary Committee had twice joined with southern Democrats to delay and weaken the legislation. On April 17, 1956, five Judiciary Republicans supported the motion by Democratic Representative Edwin E. Willis of Louisiana to recommit the pending bill to subcommittee. The motion, agreed to by a vote of 14–13, delayed committee consideration of civil rights legislation for more than a week. When the subcommittee subsequently reported back a more far-reaching bill than that favored by the Republican President Eisenhower, the Judiciary Republicans joined the southern Democrats a second time in modifying the measure.

During the consideration of the 1960 legislation, Republicans seemed bent on making ill-advised decisions. On February 5, 1959, President Eisenhower had submitted to Congress a seven-part civil rights program. Chairman

Celler then introduced legislation that went beyond the administration's proposal by calling for the development and enforcement of school desegregation plans and the creation of "Part III" powers for the Justice Department, which would have empowered the US attorney general to initiate lawsuits seeking court injunctions against anyone who deprived or was about to deprive persons of any civil right. The narrowly Democratic Senate had eliminated the Part III provision from the 1957 Civil Rights Act.

On June 17, 1959, Chairman Celler's subcommittee approved a bill that included the Eisenhower administration's proposal plus a Part III provision. The full committee, with a large measure of Republican backing, deleted the Part III provision on July 28, by an 18–13 vote and eliminated on August 4, by voice vote, the section authorizing financial aid for areas undergoing school desegregation.

Because President Eisenhower had advanced each of the deleted proposals in 1957 or 1959, active Republican support for their removal from the 1960 legislation conveyed the impression of a weakened commitment to civil rights within the Republican Party. This provided Chairman Celler with the splendid opportunity to proclaim, on August 5, 1959 (as reported the following day in the *Washington Post*), that "an unholy alliance" of southern Democrats and Republicans was responsible for removal of the school aid provision. He was quite right.

So in 1963, as civil rights legislation was again on the table, it was Celler's expectation that history would repeat itself. Should he be deprived of another opportunity to decry the "unholy alliance," he was fairly confident that liberal Republicans John Lindsay of New York, William Cahill of New Jersey, Charles Mathias of Maryland, and Clark MacGregor of Minnesota would be compelled to support the strong Democratic bill and would supply the votes needed to put that bill across in the full committee.

But what if the liberal Republicans failed to support the broad subcommittee bill? And what if the moderate and conservative Republicans failed to support southern amendments to modify the subcommittee bill? These possibilities apparently did not occur to Chairman Celler. He was certain that either the Republicans and the southern Democrats would manage to modify the measure, or enough Republicans would support the subcommittee bill to assure its approval in the full committee. Celler was confident that his strategy to scapegoat the Republicans would succeed.

* * *

Subcommittee No. 5 went into executive session on August 14, 1963, armed with the four proposals, to begin markup of a civil rights bill. In theory, a markup was a line-by-line consideration of a legislative proposal. Members weighed every word and every section of a measure to see whether these accomplished what they purported to accomplish. Generally, this was the only time in the legislative process when a measure received that kind of scrutiny. During markup of a bill, members of a subcommittee tried to dispense with partisanship and subordinate their individual predilections to the greater goal of writing a "lawyer-like" bill.

This was the ideal, anyway, and members of Congress attempted to adhere to it because of the general understanding that the subcommittee was the place to do the job. Except on major questions of great interest to the public, the work of the subcommittee was rarely overturned. Subsequently, the measure that survived the subcommittee markup was accepted, often in toto, by the full committee and approved virtually intact by the House itself.

Subcommittee No. 5 began its work at a leisurely tempo. During the initial phase of its deliberations, it performed as a model subcommittee, subjecting the various parts of the bill to exhaustive analysis. The bill was treated as the joint product of the entire subcommittee, and the announced goal of the enterprise was to report a workable, bipartisan measure.

On August 28, the subcommittee joined the nation in pausing to witness the March on Washington for Jobs and Freedom. Most members of Congress were deeply impressed by the size and demeanor of the gathering. Although many members, fearing disorder, had closed their offices for the day, a substantial number and their staff were proud to count themselves among the massive outpouring of humanity—over 200,000—that assembled at or near the Lincoln Memorial. Although the march probably did not change a single congressional vote on the bill, few Americans who were present or witnessed the televised proceedings will forget the day, especially the glorious peroration of Rev. King's "I Have a Dream" address, surely one of the most moving speeches of our time.

With August coming to a close, Deputy Attorney General Nicholas Katzenbach began a series of private discussions with Chairman Celler and Representative McCulloch on all phases of the bill; they devoted most of their attention to the explosive accommodations title. The Justice Department, acting for the White House, aimed to secure agreement on public accommodations and other features of a bill that would parallel the administration's June proposal as closely as possible yet still be acceptable to Rep. McCulloch and the Republican leadership.

House Republicans, for their part, wished to incorporate as much of the language of their January 31 and June 3 bills as the Kennedy administration would agree to include. To accomplish this, they offered a number of proposals during the subcommittee deliberations. Without Democratic support in the subcommittee, however, Republican alternatives had no chance for adoption. As I remember, Representative Toll was fond of reminding his Republican colleagues, "We've got the votes!" Nevertheless, McCulloch and fellow Republicans George Meader of Michigan, William Cramer of Florida, and Lindsay—who was sitting in as proxy for the absent Republican National Committee Chairman William Miller and thus, under the committee's rules, not a voting member—put forward a number of suggestions they believed would improve the legislation.

Meanwhile, the Leadership Conference on Civil Rights pledged that its membership would fight for the strongest bill possible. They welcomed and openly sought support for their positions from members of both parties. Although the actions of the Leadership Conference sometimes reflected a partisan Democratic tone, the conference's overriding concern was the achievement of sweeping civil rights legislation. Without bipartisan support, their goal would be unattainable.

Influential as Republican, administration, and Leadership Conference efforts might be when the bill cleared the subcommittee, their legislative goals at this stage were clearly overshadowed by the strategy of Manny Celler and the subcommittee Democrats.

As September reached its midpoint, a general aura of good feeling pervaded Subcommittee No. 5. The subcommittee continued its work and, on September 11, announced tentative approval of the least controversial provision of the president's bill: the establishment of a federal Community Relations Service. On September 12, the subcommittee also informed the press of the tentative approval of its provision for a permanent Civil Rights Commission in place of the four-year extension requested by President Kennedy.

The good feeling was misleading, for all steps taken by the subcommittee up to this point were provisional. No formal approval or disapproval had been given to a single provision or amendment to the bill—not even to the establishment of a permanent Civil Rights Commission.

And then, after September 15, everything changed.

* * *

There was a chill in the air and the skies were overcast in Birmingham, Alabama, on Sunday morning, September 15.

All over the city, people prepared for church and looked forward to a lazy Sunday dinner, a family outing, a day of rest.

It had been a turbulent month. Alabama's Governor Wallace had expressed anew his defiant opposition to court-ordered desegregation in the state's previously all-white public schools by calling up the Alabama National Guard to keep Black children from enrolling. President Kennedy had responded by federalizing the National Guard and having it step down. Above all, it had been a month during which progress in eliminating segregation had brought further anguish and turmoil for the citizens of Alabama.

The 16th Street Baptist Church, the largest Black church in Birmingham, had been the focal point and gathering place for the massive springtime demonstrations that had brought world attention to the city. Inside the building that September morning, Mrs. Ella Demand had finished leading the youngsters through the morning lesson—"The Love That Forgives" (verses 43–44 from Matthew, chapter 5). Afterwards, some of the girls left the basement classroom to go to the lounge.

Shortly before 10:30 a.m., a tremendous explosion shook the church, injuring worshippers, spewing glass, mortar, and brick, and shattering windows in nearby buildings. Under the debris that had been the girls' restroom, workmen uncovered the mangled bodies of four girls.

The city was stunned. The nation was horrified. Congress reacted sharply to the racially motivated bombing and the death of the Black children. In the House, public reaction was delayed a day; the chamber had adjourned immediately after convening on September 16, as a mark of respect for Representative Leon Gavin, Republican of Pennsylvania, who had passed away over the weekend. On the following day, Democratic Representative Roosevelt of California and Rep. Lindsay went to the well of the House to express their horror and indignation at the tragic events in Birmingham. Both saw the tragedy as a spur that should motivate Congress to act immediately on the pending civil rights legislation.

> **Mr. Roosevelt.** I hope that this tragedy will serve to remind Alabamans and all Americans of the need for the proposed civil rights legislation, so that equal rights for all Americans will become a reality, and the violence and despair engendered by the present situation will pass away forever.

> **Mr. Lindsay.** There is nothing that we legislators in Washington can say or do that will bring these little children back or that will wash away the stain of blood. But we as legislators can do our appointed task with fresh determination and conviction.
>
> That task is to draft a proper civil rights bill that is nationwide in scope and that calls upon all Americans, through our constituted Federal Government, to respect the equal protection of the laws and the full mandate of the 13th, 14th, and 15th Amendments to the Constitution. I call upon the Congress to act on legislation and to stop fiddling while the country burns.

Thus, the planning and execution of strategies—grand and otherwise—were overtaken by an unthinkable external event that affected the progress of the civil rights bill more definitively than all the songs, speeches, and pageantry of the August 28 march. The deliberations in Subcommittee No. 5 had entered a new phase.

CHAPTER 4

The Shaping and Breaking of Bipartisan Agreements
September 16–25, 1963

The Birmingham church bombing profoundly altered Subcommittee No. 5's deliberations on the civil rights bill. It quickened the pace of action and created a mood that seemed to summon forth initiative. Above all, it helped make possible a more comprehensive bill than seemed likely when President Kennedy and the House Republicans had proposed their legislation earlier in the year. Roy Wilkins, executive secretary of the NAACP, summed up the feelings of many when he told the press that the latest Birmingham outrage demonstrated the need to go beyond the present bill.

House Republicans responded to the new mood by speeding up several major efforts initiated before the church bombing. Their goal was to secure bipartisan agreement in the subcommittee on crucial provisions of the legislation. During the week of September 16, Representative McCulloch, Deputy Attorney General Katzenbach, and Representative Celler, who had been meeting informally since mid-August, arrived at the first tentative bipartisan accord on a Title II accommodations provision. The *New York Times*, in a September 18 article, announced Rep. McCulloch's approval of a compromise that would broaden the constitutional basis for Title II. The subcommittee itself made no formal announcement on accommodations, although it did inform the press that it had approved broader voting and education titles. No details of these new titles were made public.

Sometime early that week, Attorney General Robert Kennedy relayed terms of the potential accord on accommodations to Joseph Rauh Jr., counsel to the Leadership Conference on Civil Rights. According to conservative journalists Rowland Evans and Robert Novak in their syndicated column (published later, in the November 5 *New York Herald Tribune*), Rauh found the compromise impossibly weak. He also admitted, off the record, that if the compromise were passed and signed into law without being trimmed even further, he would consider it a good bill—only he could not say so publicly now.

Clarence Mitchell, Washington representative for the NAACP, learned of the agreement from Rauh and immediately sought confirmation of its existence from his friends on the Hill. Chairman Celler, who had wanted to secure the approval of the Leadership Conference before making any public announcement of the accord on accommodations, told Mitchell about the agreement and Rauh's purported approval of it, implying that Mitchell ought to take the same position. This suggestion surprised Mitchell, who had no idea that Rauh had allegedly approved the agreement. "Furious at what he took to be a sell-out, Mitchell went before the Leadership Conference full of righteous indignation," Evans and Novak wrote. "Every one of the 40 or 50 organizations represented agreed to fight the Celler compromise."

The Leadership Conference's stance effectively doomed the compromise on accommodations. Chairman Celler, partly responding to this rejection—and hoping to return to his original strategy of reporting out a strong Democratic bill from the subcommittee—informed Deputy AG Katzenbach and Rep. McCulloch that he could not support the agreement they had worked out together. He also may have felt that in the aftermath of the church bombing, compromise on the heart of the bill was as unnecessary as it was undesirable.

While McCulloch had been negotiating with Katzenbach and Celler, Representative Lindsay began discussions with Representative Richard Bolling of Missouri, a liberal Democrat and the leader of the Democratic Study Group (DSG) Task Force on Civil Rights. Rep. Bolling was the DSG's key contact man with the Leadership Conference as well as the principal civil rights spokesman on the House Rules Committee. During this period, Rep. Lindsay and

Rep. McCulloch worked independently of one another. I could tell from conversations with them that there were times when each had only the vaguest idea of what the other was doing, even as Lindsay was stepping up as an architect of the second attempt to reach an accord on public accommodations.

After Lindsay and Bolling agreed on an accommodations proposal, they discussed it with Mitchell and Rauh. Rauh suggested some acceptable revisions, and brought the proposal before the Leadership Conference on September 18 as an alternative to the Celler–McCulloch–Katzenbach compromise. The Leadership Conference quickly and enthusiastically endorsed the Lindsay–Bolling substitute Title II on accommodations, and gave Rep. Lindsay every assurance that its members would work to secure Chairman Celler's support for the proposal.

The Lindsay–Bolling approach utilized the 14th Amendment and the Commerce Clause to cover all establishments holding themselves out as doing business with the public. It read as follows:

> Sec. 201. (a) Whoever, in conducting a business of providing accommodations, amusements, entertainment, food, other goods, services or lodging to the public where such business is authorized or regulated by a state or political subdivision of a State, or the District of Columbia, or where such business engages in or affects interstate commerce, segregates or otherwise discriminates against customers on account of their race, color, religion or national origin shall be subject to suit by

the injured party in a civil action for preventive relief, including an application for a permanent or temporary injunction, restraining order, or other order.

(b) Whoever, acting under color of any law, statute, ordinance, regulation, custom or usage, requires or encourages or attempts to require or encourage the owner or operator of such business to segregate or otherwise discriminate against customers on account of their race or color, shall be subject to suit by the injured party in a civil action for preventive relief, including an application for a permanent or temporary injunction, restraining order, or other order.

On September 24, Rep. Lindsay, assured by Clarence Mitchell that Chairman Celler would agree to his amendment, attempted to offer it in the subcommittee. Celler rebuffed him, however. The reason: Lindsay was not a regular member of the subcommittee, and so could not offer an amendment. At Lindsay's request, McCulloch then offered the Lindsay–Bolling amendment. It was overwhelmingly rejected, with not only Celler but also McCulloch among those in opposition.

Chairman Celler then agreed to an amendment offered by Rep. Kastenmeier, a Democrat—one that was taken, in fact, from Kastenmeier's July bill. Though similar to the Lindsay–Bolling proposal, it lacked the bipartisan aura of the defeated amendment.

Rep. Lindsay immediately reported the result to an astonished Mitchell. Mitchell again stated that Celler had informed him of his support for the Lindsay–Bolling amendment because it had such strong backing from the Leadership Conference.

Lindsay told me later that he could not understand the failure of McCulloch, his Republican colleague, to support the amendment. He should not have been surprised, however, as he hadn't even shown McCulloch a copy of his amendment until he asked McCulloch to offer it to the subcommittee. What's more, the amendment went further in its coverage than McCulloch was prepared to go at that time. Lindsay, for his part, would have opposed the Celler–McCulloch–Katzenbach compromise if it had come to a vote, for the opposite reason: its scope was not broad enough. In the end, the failure of McCulloch and Lindsay to pursue a united course during the subcommittee deliberations merely compounded the difficulties faced by the heavily outnumbered Republicans in putting forward their alternatives to the Kennedy administration's bill.

When newspapers reported the rejection of Rep. Lindsay's amendment the following day, Chairman Celler informed members of the subcommittee—in Lindsay's absence—that he was certain Lindsay had leaked the information to the press. The charge was untrue and greatly angered Lindsay. The next time he saw Celler, Lindsay said that he was departing the subcommittee sessions permanently.

Celler had already turned down a previous request, by Democrat James Corman of California, to sit in on the subcommittee sessions. Now, genuinely annoyed with his fellow New Yorker, he declared that never again would he allow a non-subcommittee member to sit in on executive sessions of Subcommittee No. 5.

Lindsay's departure disturbed McCulloch, who believed he needed Lindsay to help him shoulder the workload of the subcommittee sessions. McCulloch also thought Celler had been unfair in his accusation about the leak. Celler, however, seemed convinced that Lindsay was departing the subcommittee sessions because his amendment had been rejected; there was no reason, he told McCulloch, why he should have supported Lindsay's proposal when McCulloch had not even done so. Of course, as McCulloch well knew, it was actually Celler's unfair charge that Lindsay had leaked information to the press—and not the defeat of Lindsay's amendment—that caused the rupture between the two New Yorkers.

Celler was being less than candid in his explanation for opposing the Lindsay–Bolling amendment on public accommodations. The reason for his action was the same as that which prompted his rejection of other Republican amendments offered during that period. Despite signals from the Justice Department and Republican members of the subcommittee, Celler had decided to return to his old strategy: load up the bill with strong Democratic language, let the Republicans and southern Democrats join forces to cut it back, and end up with legislation everyone could live with. Now, in late September—amid speculation as to why Chairman Celler had appeared to meander from his typical approach during the cooperative, pre-church-bombing phase of the subcommittee sessions, and why he had kept the subcommittee moving at such a glacial pace—the tempo of deliberations in the subcommittee hastened dramatically.

* * *

On September 24 and 25, amendments were proposed and disposed of in the subcommittee in rapid-fire succession. The Federal Employment Practices Commission bill, authored by Representative Roosevelt of California—which Chairman Powell had reported from his Committee on Education and Labor, and had threatened to bring up for House consideration by resorting to Calendar Wednesday—was offered as an amendment by Democratic Representative Peter Rodino and incorporated virtually without discussion. Yet when Representative George Meader, a Republican, suggested as a substitute the court enforcement approach, which had been favored by the Education and Labor Committee in the 87th Congress, he was given less than two minutes to discuss his idea. Chairman Celler simply said, "I think we've heard enough on that, George"—and Meader's amendment was voted down overwhelmingly.

Other Republican proposals fared as badly, while Democratic offerings were quickly adopted by the subcommittee.

The provisions of Title I (voting) were expanded to include all elections, although the presumption that any individual who had completed the sixth grade of school was literate became rebuttable in a court action. To the contrary, in the administration's bill, the presumption of literacy had been conclusive.

Rep. Kastenmeier's broad amendment expanded the number of establishments covered under Title II (public accommodations) to include every form of business establishment, including private schools, law firms, medical associations, and so forth. Under the so-called Mrs. Murphy exemption, however, owner-occupied dwellings containing five or fewer rooms for rent were excluded from the bill—and would therefore continue to be allowed to refuse tenants based on race.

Rep. Rogers's motion to add a Part III title, frequently referred to as "Title III," authorized the attorney general to institute a civil action on behalf of any individual the AG believed had been denied or deprived of rights under the Constitution or the laws of the United States by any person acting under color or appearance of law without having the legal power.

In Title IV (education), the attorney general's authority to institute or intervene in a legal action to desegregate schools was broadened to permit the AG to institute or intervene in civil actions whenever an individual complained of being denied access to or use of facilities in which any state or political subdivision was involved.

Another amendment (Title V) sharply limited the authority of the director of the Community Relations Service, while the service itself was placed within the Department of Commerce rather than, as the administration requested, the White House. This change was in response to a widely hinted White House plan to use the service to supplant and eventually replace the independent Civil Rights Commission. The commission itself, more popular with Congress than with the Kennedy administration, was made permanent in the subcommittee measure.

The power granted to federal departments and agencies to cut off federal funds upon a finding of racial discrimination in a particular program (Title VI) was changed from discretionary, as requested by the administration, to mandatory. Also as part of this provision, the attorney general would receive authority to institute civil actions compelling desegregation where federal funds were extended to states or their political subdivisions. At Rep. McCulloch's request, a state or political subdivision was given the opportunity to obtain judicial review if such funds were cut off.

On motion by Rep. Rodino, a broad FEPC provision was substituted for the section in the administration bill that gave the President's Commission on Equal Employment Opportunity (which handled government contracts) a statutory basis. This new Title VII created a National Labor Relations Board–type commission to investigate and hear all charges of discrimination in employment involving businesses, labor unions, and federal employment agencies. The commission was granted authority to hold formal hearings and to issue judicially enforceable orders. A defendant was restricted to limited review in an appellate court.

A new provision, taken from the January Republican bill, instructed the Bureau of the Census to conduct a nationwide compilation of registration and voting statistics (Title VIII), for the purpose of counting persons of voting age in every state by race, color, and national origin who were registered to vote and who had actually voted since January 1, 1960.

Another new section (Title IX) was created when Kastenmeier moved to include a provision from his July bill, which provided that any civil rights case removed to the federal court would be reviewable by appeal.

*   *   *

What was behind the shift in momentum in late September? On September 25, a potential reason became clear: the Kennedy administration's tax bill.

Until then, administration lobbyists had been suggesting the possibility of a weakened civil rights bill as an inducement to recalcitrant southern Democrats to oppose the Republican substitute on the Kennedy tax bill. Enough of them did, and the House turned down the Republican tax bill offered by Representative John Byrnes of Wisconsin, by a 199–226 vote. As soon as the battle was won, events in the subcommittee changed from a leisurely stroll to a mad dash.

On November 3, 1963, syndicated columnist Robert G. Spivack first reported that Celler had delayed the pace of the civil rights bill at the express request of the Kennedy administration. Two months later, the fuller story came out when Celler himself revealed why he had stepped on the gas. In his appearance before the House Rules Committee on January 14, 1964, Celler said, in response to questioning by Representative William Colmer, Democrat of Mississippi:

> The Administration leaders said, "We want the tax bill out first," and I said, "All right."
>
> I am guilty of dragging my feet. . . . After the tax bill was passed by the House, I then went into gear. . . . When the tax bill was out of the way, as I said, I put on the gas.

With the mad stampede of September 24–25, the mood in the subcommittee was about to change.

CHAPTER 5

The Subcommittee Reports a Bill (with Difficulty)

September 25–October 2, 1963

Subcommittee No. 5 finished its work on the civil rights bill on September 25; between then and October 2, it met to perfect the changed language. During this time, an initial attempt was made to modify the subcommittee bill. Senator Jacob Javits, Republican of New York, had previously prepared a Part III amendment that would have pinpointed the coverage to specific instances where there were denials of equal protection of the law. Despite being delivered to the committee counsel, William Foley, with a request that it be given to Chairman Celler for consideration, the Javits proposal never reached Celler. In fact, Foley decided not to show it to any of the subcommittee members. When Democratic Representative Rogers of Colorado offered the Part III amendment endorsed by the Leadership Conference on Civil Rights, he had not seen the Javits proposal.

After a phone call from Senator Javits to Celler, Celler and Rogers apparently agreed that Javits's Part III was a more suitable remedy for the specific deprivation of rights than the subcommittee provision. Rep. Rogers thereupon proposed substituting the Javits language on Part III for his own amendment.

To the surprise of everyone, Javits's substitute Part III was defeated by a 6–5 vote, with the four Republicans joined by Democrats Kastenmeier (of Wisconsin) and Toll (of Pennsylvania) in the majority. The Republicans were repaying Celler for the unfair treatment their proposals had received in the subcommittee and warning him that he could not ride over them again in the full committee. For their part, Kastenmeier and Toll voted against the substitute because they considered it a weakening amendment. A similar 6–5 vote rejected another attempt to modify the bill during this period.

Chairman Celler, though surprised and mildly concerned by this momentary revolt, was confident that Republican pique at the tactics employed in subcommittee would subside with the passage of time. Celler believed that he would be able to reestablish relations with Rep. McCulloch and, through him, with the Republican leadership. This was essential for the success of his strategy.

As a result of Celler's approach, the tentative decisions made by the subcommittee during the "stampede" phase of the subcommittee deliberations were now frozen into the bill as it moved to the full committee.

Clearly, all the subcommittee's Republicans were still angry at the way they had been treated in Chairman Celler's subcommittee. Rep. Lindsay had already walked out of the subcommittee sessions in response to Celler's false charge that he had leaked information to the press. Meanwhile, Rep. McCulloch was perturbed at the high-handed way he and the other subcommittee Republicans had been treated when they offered amendments to the bill on September 24 and 25 or sought time to speak on the strengthening amendments rammed through by the subcommittee Democrats. His thwarting of Celler's efforts to "clean up" the language of the bill was a direct response to Celler's steamroller tactics. Republican National Committee Chairman William Miller, however, said nothing.

When filing their views on the legislation in the committee report, Rep. Meader of Michigan and Rep. Cramer of Florida—the other Republican members of the subcommittee—wrote accounts of how they had been treated. Although he was an opponent of civil rights legislation, Cramer offered the following fair account:

Hearings were held on this bill until August when subcommittee markup of the bill commenced. This proceeded for about 6 weeks until September 25, 1963, the day the vote on the tax bill took place, and every indication was given until then that the [civil rights] bill would be considered on an impartial, bipartisan basis and in an attempt to write as good a bill as possible.

When the tax bill was passed, the mood and modus operandi noticeably changed. The majority on the subcommittee submitted previously prepared amendments, many of which had not been theretofore considered; they were crammed through and a much stronger bill emerged than the very strong bill recommended by the administration.

Rep. Meader tendered a more detailed statement in the committee report on the events that occurred during the subcommittee's hectic final consideration of the civil rights bill:

At the outset of these sessions a question of committee policy was raised (by the undersigned); namely, whether it would be the objective of the subcommittee to produce a well-worded, workable bill which stood a chance of becoming law without major modification or whether it would be our purpose to add to the bill controversial provisions which could be sloughed off as trading material during the legislative process.

After discussion, the subcommittee agreed it would not load up the bill but would try to write a clearly-worded and workable bill which stood a good chance of becoming law.

On this basis the subcommittee proceeded to consider the provisions of the Administration bill in nonpartisan, largely unanimous action, modifying the language title by title, page by page, line by line, arriving at tentative decisions on phraseology, and agreeing on items which required further information and further study . . .

The subcommittee had arrived at tentative decisions on the phraseology on all the titles of H.R. 7152 at the time the tax reduction bill, H.R. 8363, was being debated on the floor of the House.

At that time a curious change in the atmosphere of subcommittee consideration abruptly took place. Nonpartisan harmony evaporated. A rigidity of position based on the possession of an overwhelming majority of votes (seven Democrats to four Republicans) prevailed. . . . Alternatives to titles and sections were rejected out of hand, and three explosively controversial provisions were added:

(1) H.R. 405, the so-called FEPC bill, reported by the House Education and Labor Committee, then pending before the Rules Committee.

(2) A broad Title III vesting sweeping powers in the Attorney General to initiate and to intervene in any case to enforce rights derived from the Constitution or laws of the United States.

(3) A broadening of the public accommodations section of title II to extend its coverage to practically every type of business.

Thus modified the subcommittee reported the bill to the full Judiciary Committee on October 2.

The merits of these new provisions . . . were never debated in the subcommittee.

When the subcommittee reported the bill on October 2, the action shifted to the full Judiciary Committee. Under Chairman Celler's direction, Subcommittee No. 5 had reported a strong bill that satisfied civil rights groups—but it was an overwhelmingly Democratic bill that was substantially unacceptable to the subcommittee Republicans, who had been rebuffed in most of their efforts to amend it.

Failing to reflect even approximately the alliances and configurations of the full Judiciary Committee or the House itself, Subcommittee No. 5 had afforded its liberal Democrats the opportunity to advance legislation that lacked sufficient support for the arduous congressional journey. Furthermore, since no southern Democratic opponent of civil rights legislation was a member of Subcommittee No. 5, any bill it proposed was unlikely to pass muster among the most stubborn opponents of civil rights legislation.

Taking the broad view, fully *100* members of the House of Representatives had been denied representation in drafting a measure whose primary thrust would be felt in their own congressional districts. Admittedly, most southern Democrats and some conservative Republicans were opposed to civil rights legislation in any form. Yet to draft a bill without at least some participation by those members of Congress from regions most affected by its contents seemed hardly in the spirit of civil rights.

In my view, either the full committee or a select committee of the House would have been more suitable for the monumental task entrusted to Subcommittee No. 5. The Ways and Means Committee, for example, considered almost all legislation as a full committee. What it accomplished regularly with 25 members, the House Judiciary Committee could have accomplished this one time with 35.

The benefits of assigning such critical legislation to a select committee appointed specially for the task were well known. In fact, there was historical precedent for a select committee approach. During the debate on the Compromise of 1850, crucial measures referred to select committees of the House and Senate included those providing for the admission of California to the Union, enacting a new Fugitive Slave Law, abolishing the slave trade in the District of Columbia, funding the Texas debt, settling the Texas–New Mexico boundary dispute, and establishing territorial governments in New Mexico and Utah.

Comprising many of the ablest people in Congress, these committees reflected the great divisions of public sentiment on questions that threatened to dissolve the Union. The civil rights revolution of the 1960s demanded no less.

To compound the difficulties, the Judiciary Committee lacked proper jurisdiction over many separate provisions of the bill. Legislation on voting, Part III, the Civil Rights Commission, and the remand of civil rights cases were indeed subjects correctly in the committee's domain. Yet other existing House committees had more experience and expertise in coping with some of the matters dealt with so speedily in Subcommittee No. 5 and about to face resolution in the full committee.

Public accommodations arguably belonged more appropriately in the Interstate and Foreign Commerce Committee. Title IV belonged to Education and Labor. Legislation creating a Community Relations Service was more properly the province of the Government Operations Committee. Ways and Means, or Banking and Currency, might have claimed authority regarding the cutting off of federal financial assistance. The topic of Equal Employment Opportunity habitually received consideration only in the Education and Labor Committee. Title VIII, on registration and voting statistics, would have been referred automatically to the Census Subcommittee of the Post Office and Civil Services Committee.

On these matters, the expertise of the Judiciary Committee members and the committee staff was arguably inferior to that possessed by the members and staffs of these other committees. Nevertheless, because the comprehensive civil rights legislation was presented in an omnibus measure, it followed in the tradition of being referred to the Judiciary Committee alone.

In addition, Subcommittee No. 5 never adequately considered many of the provisions adopted so hastily on September 24 and 25. Parts of the bill were rushed through the subcommittee without adequate discussion or opportunity for amendments. These actions hardly constituted proper subcommittee consideration of such significant legislation.

The initial strategies of compromise had broken down. The failure of Rep. McCulloch and Deputy AG Katzenbach to persuade Chairman Celler to continue his support of their public accommodations compromise was matched by the failure of Rep. Lindsay, Rep. Bolling, and the Leadership Conference to secure Celler's support for an amendment that normally he would have found acceptable. The short shrift Celler accorded the Republican amendments were sure to have severe repercussions in the full committee.

Yet Chairman Celler stood his ground. Twice on the verge of supporting bipartisan compromise, Celler had returned to the strategy with which he felt most comfortable: positioning himself as the heroic martyr overwhelmed by the superior numbers of the unholy alliance of Republicans and southern Democrats. Despite the assertions of many commentators, Celler did not capitulate to the power of the civil rights groups; his failure to support a Leadership Conference–backed accommodations proposal was clear evidence of his independence of these groups. His strategy was his own, based on his hope that history would repeat itself. It had worked in 1957 and had been a triumph of legislative wizardry in 1960. Celler was sure it would work again.

But the success of Celler's strategy depended on the existence of a genuine working relationship—a true coalition—between southern Democrats and Republicans. What Celler and so many others did not realize was that this old coalition no longer existed. With the presence of a strengthened Republican Party in the South, the ties of cooperation that had prevailed for so many years were loosening as Republicans sought to unseat the very men they had worked with harmoniously in the past. At every level, from the courthouse to the halls of Congress, the Republicans were challenging and, in some in instances, successfully unseating southern Democrats.

The new mood was felt in the House Judiciary Committee. In 1956, 1957, and 1959, southern Republicans Rep. Cramer of Florida and Rep. Poff of Virginia had joined their Democratic committee colleagues in approving the minority views on civil rights bills. In 1963, they were to write their own separate views on the civil rights legislation. Manny Celler had overlooked something, and this proved ruinous to his plan. He saw only two alternatives for the Republicans: They could vote for the southern Democrat–sponsored amendments to modify the bill, as they had in 1956 and 1959, and earn the opprobrium of the civil rights groups. Or a sufficiently large number of them could stick with the subcommittee bill and provide it with the bare majority necessary to clear the full committee.

What Celler did not consider, and what was so dramatically demonstrated to him during the final days of the subcommittee sessions, was that the Republicans would adopt *neither* alternative. As it turned out, they would not only oppose all efforts to modify the subcommittee bill—which, as Celler knew, had to be modified or face disaster on the floor of the House (if not first in the full committee, without ever reaching the House floor)—but also withhold support for the subcommittee measure itself.

It should have been clear to Chairman Celler that a successful legislative effort on civil rights had to be not just bipartisan, but so overwhelmingly bipartisan that it would withstand assaults both in the committee and on the House floor. Quite simply, it had to be kept away from the arena of political controversy. The legislation had to be rock-solid in order to withstand the worst of political storms looming beyond the Capitol. It had to be safeguarded from becoming an explosive subject in the next election or an issue that would create an even more divisive impact on American life. And there was only one way to do that.

The bill had to be thoroughly bipartisan.

Despite the still-raw memory of the 16th Street Baptist Church bombing in Birmingham and the deaths of four girls, the first stage of enacting meaningful civil rights legislation—trying to draft legislation in Celler's Subcommittee No. 5—had failed to produce a bipartisan approach. That led to the next challenge: Could the full Judiciary Committee draft a bipartisan civil rights bill and thus succeed where the subcommittee had failed?

In the early days of October 1963, this was the vital question observers and participants were asking themselves.

CHAPTER 6

Chaos in the Full Committee
October 7–14, 1963

While awaiting its fate in the new civil rights bill, the Civil Rights Commission—established back in 1957 when Congress passed the first civil rights act of the century—was about to go out of business. On October 7, however, after a debate on the House floor, the commission's life was extended. The Senate had added a one-year extension as an amendment to a private claims bill, which had already passed the House, providing $816.83 in retroactive death benefits to a soldier's widow, Elizabeth G. Mason of Moulton, Massachusetts. The bill, with the amendment, passed the Senate easily, 70–15, after a lackluster discussion punctuated by Georgia Democrat Richard Russell's brief comment on the commission: "Let it die!"

Despite southern Democrats' vigorous denunciation of the commission in the House, the vote there on the resolution agreeing to the bill and amendment was 265–80. The Democrats voted 136–71 (66 percent) in favor; the Republican vote was 129–9 (93 percent).

It was unclear, however, what the House Democratic leaders were up to that day. According to the October 3 whip notice of Republican Representative Les Arends of Illinois, listing the official House program for the following week, the Consent Calendar (which would allow noncontroversial bills to proceed without debate) was to have been called first. Instead, Democratic Speaker John McCormack of Massachusetts and House Judiciary Committee Chairman Celler—after consulting House Parliamentarian Lew Deschler, but without telling the Republican leaders—brought the bill and amendment to the House floor before the Consent Calendar was called.

As a result, no Republican Judiciary Committee members were on the House floor when the session began. By default, Republican Representative H. R. Gross of Iowa, who was routinely in the Chamber to object to unanimous Consent Calendar bills, controlled the 20 minutes allotted to the House Republicans. He yielded most of the time to southern Democrats, allowing Ohio's McCulloch, when he arrived, only three minutes. The southerners were in good humor, especially Representative Elijah "Tic" Forrester of Georgia. New York's Lindsay was the only supporter of the Civil Rights Commission to reply to the diatribes leveled by southern representatives against the commission.

Why had the House Democrats brought the bill and its provocative amendment to the House floor without consulting the Republicans? Was something afoot between the northern and southern Democrats?

The full Judiciary Committee got off to an unsettling, even perplexing start when it considered the subcommittee bill the next day, October 8. Bill Foley, the committee counsel, began to read the bill. I was told later that as Chairman Celler started a lengthy explanation of it, he was interrupted by all sorts of questions and disagreements. The proceedings ended when the House convened and Democratic Representative Willis of Louisiana, invoking the rule against committee meetings while the House was in session, objected to continuing.

Rep. McCulloch asked me to come to his office that afternoon to work on a statement objecting to the subcommittee version of the bill. While I was there, he took a call from Speaker McCormack. I could hardly believe what I heard.

It seemed that a new harmonious spirit existed between the GOP and Democratic leaders. They actually had a plan to modify the bill. Rep. Willis was going to offer an amendment the next day to restrict coverage of the voting rights title (Title I) to federal elections only. This was going to happen with the blessing of both Chairman Celler and Speaker McCormack—shades of 1956, 1957, and 1959–60 all over again. I didn't know how this new accord was reached, but I suspected it came about after the previous day's debate on the Civil Rights Commission. I wasn't entirely sure who was involved in this new agreement, but Celler, McCulloch, McCormack, Halleck, and Willis certainly were. Halleck had probably talked tough to McCormack.

When McCulloch said goodbye to McCormack and hung up the phone, he could see I was surprised. He asked what troubled me. I told him that the Republicans wouldn't—and shouldn't—support a southern Democratic move to modify the bill.

"Celler got us into this mess," I said. "He should get us out." Although a moderate bill would stand a better chance of getting out of the Judiciary Committee and being accepted by a majority in the full House, I knew that Republicans didn't want to end up being blamed for modifications and portrayed as opposing civil rights.

Rep. McCulloch replied that he would think about what I said, but I realized I had not convinced him that it would be a bad move to join southern Democrats in weakening the legislation.

As I was leaving McCulloch's office, I saw Rep. Cramer in the corridor. Cramer told me that he knew what was up—that he and Rep. Poff had learned about it from southern Democrats during the Judiciary Committee session. He seemed angry and said he was going to talk to McCulloch. He added, "Manny Celler has set a trap for the Republicans. If we run true to form, we'll fall right into it. He wants us to be the goats in cutting back a bill we had nothing to do with strengthening in the first place."

I returned to my office and spoke to Bill Copenhaver, who said he was sure something was up but it was not his place as minority counsel to talk to Rep. McCulloch. I replied that I had spoken to McCulloch and that Rep. Cramer was speaking to him "right now." I then called Rep. Lindsay and Rep. Mathias of Maryland, both of whom were upset; they were prepared to spread the word among their colleagues to stand firm against the Willis Title I voting amendment. Apparently, among the Republican Judiciary Committee members, only McCulloch had been consulted on the new agreement.

There was great concern over what was likely to happen.

Phone calls and meetings persuaded most of the committee Republicans to oppose the Willis amendment when it was offered. Communications problems were immensely complicated by the absence of three Republican committee members who were away on official business. Representative Arch Moore of West Virginia and Representative Clark MacGregor of Minnesota were at a convention in Geneva, Switzerland, on the topic of refugee problems. Representative Cahill of New Jersey was on a committee trip to South America. Rep. Lindsay moved swiftly, however, and obtained the proxies of Cahill and MacGregor from their respective assistants, Eugenia Daugherty and Stan Langland.

The Judiciary Committee meeting the next morning, October 9, was acrimonious. Sharp charges and counter-charges of partisanship filled the committee room—room 346 of the Cannon Building—reflecting the chaos that surrounded the legislation. After the hubbub subsided, a lackluster session on Title I concluded the meeting. No amendments were offered.

Immediately after the committee meeting, Rep. Lindsay and I returned to his office. His administrative assistant,

Marion Clow, seemed amused. "You have a visitor," she said cheerfully. Lindsay and I entered his private office and there, seated at Lindsay's desk, was Representative Clarence Brown of Ohio, senior Republican on the House Rules Committee.

"Hello, John," boomed Representative Brown's familiar voice. "Sit down! What can I do for you?" he joked.

They wasted no time in small talk. Brown quickly informed Lindsay that he was aware of the secret agreement between the the Republican and Democratic leaders to cut back the civil rights bill in committee. He warned Lindsay of the dire consequences the GOP would face if it went along with any southern Democratic amendments.

"Our so-called statesmen," Brown continued, referring to McCulloch and Minority Leader Halleck, "seem to enjoy all their hobnobbing with the elite around here and the big shots downtown. They ought to know we're going to get all the blame and none of the credit on this bill. The condescension of those civil rights and labor boys is a thing of beauty. Oh, they'll bow and scrape for our votes now! But if you met them on the street the day after the bill gets through the House, they wouldn't know you from the nearest manhole, and it won't be long before they'll get back to calling you the old names they used to."

Lindsay said he agreed with Brown and would do whatever was necessary to avoid the mousetrap.

Brown urged Lindsay to call him whenever he felt like it, saying, "You boys better stand firm on this. The Democrats have to show some good faith before we bail them out."

Rep. Lindsay was aware of the significance of Rep. Brown's visit. He knew that Republican members of the Rules Committee were likely to follow Brown's lead when and if a measure was reported out of the Judiciary Committee.

Rep. Brown's involvement was significant in a deeper sense, too, as he was bearing up under a heavy personal load. Badly crippled by arthritis, and bowed by the fatal illness of his daughter and the serious incapacitation of his beloved wife, he had nonetheless taken an active interest in the struggle over the civil rights bill.

The subject of the Brown–Lindsay discussion was renewed later in the day at a secret session of the House Republican Policy Committee. Presumably, the meeting had been called at the request of the Republican leadership to ratify their agreement with McCormack and Celler to modify the bill. Representative Tom Curtis of Missouri described the meeting to me afterwards: Halleck and McCulloch, with qualified support from Republican Representative and GOP Congressional Campaign Committee Chairman Bob Wilson of California, defended their decision to seek agreement with the Kennedy administration and the Judiciary Committee Democrats as the only way to secure a workable civil rights bill.

Their position was sharply disputed by Rep. Curtis, Rep. Brown, Rep. Arends (the Republican Party whip), Rep. John Byrnes of Wisconsin, Rep. Gerald Ford of Michigan, and a substantial majority of the House Judiciary Republicans. These members, while commending the objective of Minority Leader Halleck and Rep. McCulloch to reach across the aisle and support strong civil rights legislation, strongly differed with them over the means they had chosen to achieve that goal. Halleck and McCulloch were apparently willing to work with southern Democrats in changing the language of the bill. But Brown, Arends, Ford, and the others argued that the biggest blunder the House Republicans could make would be to vote for a southern Democratic amendment to weaken the legislation.

"You know how simple-minded everybody is on this," Rep. Curtis said to me. "The amendment could be the Lord's Prayer or the Ten Commandments, but as long as a southern Democrat is going to offer it, we have to oppose it. If we do otherwise, we will be roasted for trying to gut the bill. This is going to be true as long as people are more interested in who offered the amendment than in what the amendment says. Our only recourse is to insist that Manny Celler offer all amendments to the bill."

After a lengthy discussion, Rep. Curtis explained, those at the secret meeting had considered what could be done to force the Democrats to assume responsibility for undoing what they had done in the subcommittee. Some members suggested inviting Attorney General Robert Kennedy to reappear before the Judiciary Committee and putting the onus on him and the administration for modifying the bill. Everyone at the meeting received this suggestion enthusiastically. But there was one stipulation: The request should be put by Chairman Celler on behalf of the entire committee. Only if Celler refused to request the attorney general's return to the committee would a motion be made in the committee to direct him to do so.

Rep. McCulloch was asked to inform Celler of the sense of the meeting that day. On the morning of October 10, McCulloch met secretly with Deputy AG Katzenbach first. He explained that Republicans would strongly resist any amendments offered by southern Democrats to modify the bill. He also advised Katzenbach of the Republican decision to request that the attorney general return to the committee to give the administration's views on the subcommittee bill.

Immediately afterwards, McCulloch and Katzenbach went to the House Speaker's office, where they met with Speaker McCormack, Minority Leader Halleck, Majority Leader Carl Albert of Oklahoma, and Chairman Celler. McCulloch and Halleck told those present of the Republicans' adverse reaction to the agreement the joint leadership had reached some days before. They urged Celler to invite the attorney general to return or risk being forced to do so by motion of the Judiciary Committee. Celler agreed to announce it at the end of the next meeting of the full committee.

Subsequently, Celler and Katzenbach asked Representative Roland Libonati, Democrat of Illinois, to offer the amendment that Representative Willis had been planning to offer. Assuming that the Kennedy administration, Celler, and the Judiciary Republicans would all support the amendment, Representative Libonati agreed to be its author. In this way, the northern Democrats could allay Republican fears by a demonstration that they were now prepared to take the initiative in undoing some of the handiwork of the Democrat-leaning subcommittee.

As soon as the Judiciary Committee meeting began on October 10, Rep. Libonati offered the amendment to cut back the coverage of the voting provisions to federal elections only. Democratic Representative William Tuck of Virginia followed with an amendment to strike out the entirety of Title I. This succession of events created an impression that Rep. Tuck had offered the southern Democratic amendment while Libonati was acting for the administration and the committee's northern Democrats. But was this a ploy for an eventual trade-off?

Suspecting a trap, Rep. Cramer began to question the amendments. He was still interrogating the authors when it was time for the session to end. Chairman Celler then announced that upon the request of members of both parties, Attorney General Kennedy would be invited back to testify before the full committee. The committee adjourned until Tuesday, October 15, when it would hear the attorney general.

Later that afternoon, according to the scuttlebutt, the committee's northern Democrats met to discuss their next move, but reached no agreement, as they had difficulty fathoming the moves and intentions of the committee Republicans.

Meanwhile, the Lindsay–Celler feud continued to flare. Rep. Lindsay wrote Celler a letter complaining that the printed transcripts of the committee hearings, which had just been issued, were published without an index. He also charged that the bills included in the first volume of transcripts were almost useless because they omitted the names of the representatives submitting them. The committee staff were upset when they learned of the errors; blame was affixed everywhere.

The source of the trouble soon became clear: The Judiciary Committee staff had merely copied the format of previous transcripts on civil rights hearings, without questioning whether the old way of doing things was at all adequate. Although this seemed like a minor issue, it was further evidence that Chairman Celler and his staff were treating the 1963 civil rights legislative process as if it were simply a rerun of the 1957 and 1960 fights—a struggle in which he and the Democrats were destined to come out on top.

* * *

During a lunch on October 11 with John Beckler of the Associated Press (AP) and Arnold Sawislak of United Press International (UPI), I asked their views on the Libonati amendment. They said that if the amendment was on the level and received the support of Celler and the Kennedy administration, then Republicans might be able to support it and thus produce a break in the impasse threatening the bill's progress in the House.

Many people did not realize that journalists with the experience and savvy of Beckler and Sawislak played a significant role in the shaping of legislation. Their suggestions, reports, intelligence, fears, and uncertainties were taken very seriously by members of Congress. Their sense of mood, many contacts, and wide vantage points were greatly respected by the actors in the legislative drama.

Often during the long months of House consideration of the civil rights bill, members of the press brought crucial information to the attention of those of us working on the legislation. Catherine Mackin of the 18-newspaper Hearst Headline Service, for example, frequently shared with me pertinent views of the attorney general. For our part, Bill Copenhaver and I were frank with journalists, telling them everything we could without betraying confidences. We never deliberately misled them. In return, they were candid in their advice to us and fair in their presentation of the news. The collaboration between reporters and participants was of crucial significance to the legislative process.

Copenhaver and I dubbed Beckler and Sawislak the co-chairmen of the "Rat Pack," so named because these journalists often traveled together, covering the civil rights bill in the House from directly on the scene. They trudged through corridors, sat in committee rooms, waited in offices to catch the fast-breaking events—and often learned of happenings before the principals themselves did. They were active pursuers of the news who, in contrast with some of their colleagues (except the columnists), learned everything by telephone, direct pipeline, or backstage whisper.

The journalists of the Rat Pack won the respect of congressional staffers. They did their job with dedication, patience, and great professional skill. Although we did not and could not be expected to agree with everything they wrote, we never doubted their sense of fairness and proportion. We never questioned their willingness to present issues in all their complexity.

In addition to Beckler, Sawislak, and Mackin, another Rat Pack regular was E. W. Kenworthy of the *New York Times*, who on occasion replaced Anthony Lewis in covering the bill—to the relief of almost everyone except perhaps the Department of Justice, as the latter always sided with it. Andy Glass of the *New York Herald Tribune*, Richard Lyons of the *Washington Post*, John Averill of the *Los Angeles Times*, Peter Kumpa of the *Baltimore Sun*, Bob Walsh of the *Washington Star*, Robert Semple of the *New York Times* (formerly of the *National Observer*), and Joe Sullivan of the *Wall Street Journal* were also familiar faces on the Hill.

The most influential of the syndicated columnists during the civil rights fight included Joseph Alsop, Charles Bartlett, Roscoe Drummond, Rowland Evans and Robert Novak, Doris Fleeson, Arthur Krock, David Lawrence, Walter Lippmann, Drew Pearson, Mary McGrory, James Reston, and William White. Cartoonists such as Herbert "Herblock" Block, Bill Mauldin, Paul Conrad, and Charles Brooks also made their impact felt throughout deliberations on the bill.

No committee meeting was held on the following Monday, October 14, and little had changed over the weekend. That day, I spoke with David Cohen of Americans for Democratic Action (ADA), Clarence Mitchell of the NAACP, and Bill Phillips of the Democratic Study Group. Everyone was curious about what would happen with the Libonati amendment to limit voting rights to federal elections only. I spent a lot of time that week with NAACP's Mitchell in particular, warning him that if the Libonati amendment were approved, this fight would only get nastier and more partisan. Mitchell said he was worried but didn't think it would pass. He hoped the Republicans would stand firm against the anticipated appeal by the attorney general to modify the bill.

Anthony Lewis had a big piece on the bill that same day in the *New York Times,* which disturbed civil rights leaders because it depicted them as naive, quixotic, and potentially destructive while it painted the Kennedy administration as wise and statesmanlike. A headline for the Lewis piece, GOP UNLIKELY TO SUPPORT STIFF MEASURE OF HOUSE JUDICIARY SUBCOMMITTEE, was totally misleading, as most of the committee Republicans were prepared to stick with the subcommittee bill unless and until northern Democrats moved to modify it. I wondered why Lewis had ignored the Libonati amendment in his article. After all, he surely knew it was the pending business before the committee.

Wondering if the Libonati amendment was meant to be a trap for them, House Republicans remained suspicious of it and would remain so unless it received Democratic support. So far, none had materialized. Everyone was waiting to hear what the attorney general would say.

CHAPTER 7

The Attorney General Returns to the Judiciary Committee
October 15–16, 1963

Attorney General Robert Kennedy appeared before the House Judiciary Committee on the morning of October 15 to represent the administration's views on Subcommittee No. 5's recent handiwork. The session was closed to the public, but Rep. Lindsay and Bill Copenhaver filled me in on what happened. The attorney general had prepared a statement, in which he once again endorsed the administration's June bill and called for prompt bipartisan action:

I am here today to support the legislation which the President submitted. . . .

A strong civil rights bill can only be enacted if this committee and this Congress put aside partisan considerations and both political parties work together toward that end. Conviction as to the need for comprehensive legislation and belief in the rightness of the cause is no monopoly to either party.

Legislation will result if Republicans and Democrats work together in this committee, in the Rules Committee, and on the floor of the House. Differences as to approach and emphasis must not be permitted to be escalated into the arena of politics—or the country will be the loser.

AG Kennedy's statement was polite and conciliatory as he reviewed various changes the subcommittee had made to the administration's June bill. Kennedy opposed the change in Title I that required the impounding of ballots cast by persons found qualified to vote under the temporary referee procedure (which the president had introduced in his February version) because it would delay counting votes of qualified voters and make the outcome of elections uncertain. Regarding Title II, he disapproved of the general invocation of the 14th Amendment and called for a specific delineation of the public establishments that would be covered under the accommodations title. He flatly opposed the new civil injunctive authority granted to the attorney general under Title III because it would inject federal executive power into areas that were not the administration's legitimate concern. He also disagreed with limiting the number of employees of the Community Relations Service to six.

The attorney general also expressed his strong support of a fair employment practices provision, either as part of the civil rights bill; as an amendment to the bill on the floor of the House, in the event that Rules Committee opposition to an employment provision would jeopardize chances for a rule on the omnibus bill; or as separate legislation to be enacted following passage of the omnibus bill.

He did not address a number of other important changes in the bill.

In the discussion that followed, there were no clashes between the AG and Rep. Lindsay, who hardly spoke at all. The session was over in a couple of hours, as the committee did not obtain the necessary unanimous consent of the House to meet while the chamber was in session. Questioning of AG Kennedy, therefore, was relatively brief and he was scheduled to return the next day.

After the session, Rep. McCulloch said to me that the attorney general had made "very useful, very constructive suggestions, some that I would make and have been making."

Rep. Lindsay said, "I think it was helpful that he came up."

On the other hand, Clarence Mitchell of the NAACP was far from happy. Reiterating charges that he had made in speeches throughout the month, Mitchell said, "There is no reason for this sellout. The administration should be in there fighting for the subcommittee bill. Instead, the attorney general is trying to get the people who are committed to it to change their position."

Two problems continued to bother me. I didn't know how the attorney general could speak of bipartisanship without acknowledging Republican positions. What he seemed to be suggesting or implying was a definition of bipartisanship that called simply for the House Republicans to support the Democratic administration. That wasn't genuine bipartisanship and certainly wouldn't break the impasse.

Equally vexing was AG Kennedy's position on the Libonati amendment restricting coverage of the voting title to federal elections. His statement to the committee seemed to offer something to both sides:

> The first [subcommittee] change [from the president's original proposal] has been to make these provisions applicable to State as well as Federal elections. This change eliminates one of the constitutional bases for the legislation, since the power of Congress under Article I, section 4, of the Constitution extends only to the regulation of Federal elections. These provisions of the bill would, however, still be supported by the 14th and 15th amendments. In my view, therefore, they would be constitutional even as applied to State elections.
>
> Others do not share my views in this regard. Their doubts both as to the constitutionality and the wisdom of Federal regulation of State elections could impede passage of the bill. It was for this reason, and because we believe that the legislation would be effective whether or not State elections were covered, that the bill we proposed was confined to Federal elections.

It seemed that the attorney general supported the Libonati amendment for practical reasons but didn't want to say so in so many words because, I thought, he was reluctant to incur additional wrath from the civil rights groups. Surely he did not want to take direct responsibility for the first major amendment cutting back the bill in the full committee.

In fact, the first question Kennedy received—from Democrat Byron Rogers of Colorado—went right to the subject of the Libonati amendment.

> **Mr. Rogers.** Mr. Attorney General, I take from your statement as it relates to Title I that as you outlined, the subcommittee has changed it from Federal to State elections [as well] and you have no particular objection to that kind of a change?
>
> **Attorney General Kennedy.** I have no objection to it. I would want to make sure that we do not lose supporters of Title I as it was originally introduced because of the inclusion of State elections.

So the attorney general's support for the amendment seemed to turn on whether its inclusion would strengthen or diminish support for the bill.

The Judiciary Committee had sought AG Kennedy's views because it was unsure of what to do. Was the attorney general simply handing the question back to the committee? That's what it looked like.

In my journal for October 15, I wrote the following:

Just back from the Eisenhower birthday dinner, a gala affair at the Shoreham Hotel. Went with PR man Freddy Sontag. Met David Broder of the *Star*. Spoke with Stan Langland of MacGregor's office and Republican Reps. Hastings Keith of Massachusetts and John Rhodes of Arizona. Keith and Rhodes said they were getting lots of favorable civil rights mail. Rhodes bluntly said he wished Lindsay "were more of a team man and less a demagogue." A bit brutally put, I think. Rhodes and Melvin Laird, leaders of the Conservative wing of the party, are tough and shrewd. Rhodes seems to think everyone ought to stay in line.

I said hello to Sen. Hugh Scott. An inebriated lady in a strapless gown and much jewelry was being loud and obstreperous and resistant to efforts to calm her. Ethel Merman was here to sing. She stood very close to me before she went on and looked surprisingly nervous. Lately she has not been in terrific voice, certainly not since her great performance in *Gypsy*. But tonight, she was at her best.

The attorney general continued in the committee throughout the day of October 16. There was heavy questioning on a variety of subjects, mostly from the southerners, and perhaps they made slight headway. The climate around the bill seemed a little less partisan, but there was still no discernible progress.

Chairman Celler began the session that day with a prepared statement. He said he would set aside his personal feelings with regard to the provisions added in the subcommittee and would support a bill along the lines recommended by the administration. In asking both liberal Democrats and Republicans to support the administration bill, which the subcommittee had greatly strengthened, Celler said:

> The statement with respect to civil rights legislation made yesterday by the Attorney General and his testimony today before the committee have done much to clarify the administration's position with respect to the bill recommended by the subcommittee. The Attorney General stressed the need for legislation without further delay, as well as the necessity for bipartisan support for civil rights in Congress.
>
> The administration proposes a strong civil rights bill and one that I feel both Democrats and Republicans can support. The urgency for bipartisan legislation at this session is so strong that I intend to put aside my own feelings with respect to the desirability of provisions in addition to those recommended by the administration. I shall exert every effort toward achieving a bill along the lines recommended by the administration to be reported out of this committee within two weeks.

Celler's brand of bipartisanship, it seemed, was akin to the administration's: *Let's get together and do what I want to do.* It seemed to me that Celler may have forfeited the Republican members' trust altogether.

When I spoke later with Bill Pitts, the administrative assistant in Rep. Arends's office, he was cynical. "I urge you to get a statement out to the press denouncing the administration's charade," he said. "When all's said and done, they still want us to do the dirty work and cut back the bill." The administration was obviously concerned that a strong bill would face fierce opposition in both the House and Senate, and wanted the Republicans to take responsibility for weakening it.

I saw Arends briefly, and he tossed me a bag of peanuts, saying, "We've got a big vote coming up. Can't you arrange a speaking engagement for Lindsay, to get him out of town so at least we don't have to worry about him voting against us?"

At noon, Clarence Mitchell was outside the committee room denouncing "the sellout behind closed doors." "Everybody in there is a white man," he commented bitterly to journalists gathered there. After Mitchell finished speaking to the press, he said, "Come on, Bob! Get the Republicans to speak out against the Libonati amendment and this whole move to cut back the subcommittee bill."

Later in the day, Mitchell seemed more encouraged. He told me the committee Democrats were not rallying to support the Libonati amendment. Meanwhile, Lindsay said he thought the Republicans would split on it, but added, "We can't be sure how they'll go."

I talked to Copenhaver, who said that AG Kennedy had really mixed everybody up on the Libonati amendment, shading his answers differently to suit whoever was questioning him. For example, Copenhaver said, he gave totally divergent answers to Democratic Reps. Willis (of Louisiana) and Kastenmeier (of Wisconsin).

Confirmation of the attorney general's failure to take a clear position was borne out by the transcript of the day's session:

Mr. Willis. I take it that you are now recommending to the committee that Title I be restricted to Federal elections?

Attorney General Kennedy. Well, my feeling on that, Congressman, is, as I stated yesterday, that I think that it does what we need to have done by restricting it to Federal elections. There is a feeling by the subcommittee that it should encompass State elections as well. I don't think that that is necessary. But I wouldn't oppose it; we wouldn't oppose it if it were contained in the legislation. I think that is up to the committee to determine how that should be handled. I think that the statement I have made yesterday is that what we need and what we would like is legislation modeled after what the President recommended.

Now, that doesn't mean that what we are looking for is to have it reported out exactly as the President suggested. I am sure that it can be improved, and I think with consultation between Republicans and Democrats that it can be improved.

Mr. Willis. I understand your position.

Attorney General Kennedy. But that is one of the areas, Federal and State elections, that I would expect would be discussed by those who are interested in having some legislation.

Mr. Willis. And I know that there will be discussions by the committee while you are here, and I know of course that you would accept provisions added to the bill. But taking all the factors involved, everything involved, you would recommend that that be done, that it be restricted to Federal elections? I am trying to be specific, I must confess.

Attorney General Kennedy. If it is the feeling on the part of those who want to be associated with the legislation that it should be confined to Federal elections, I would be glad to suggest that it be confined to Federal elections. I just don't have the feeling of the members of the committee who are actually interested in obtaining legislation, Congressman. I am not trying to avoid it. I would be glad, if you could tell me now that there was a strong feeling by several members of the committee who would otherwise support the legislation, but have a real concern about the State elections being included; I would be glad to say I don't think State elections should be included.

I don't think it is necessary to the bill, Congressman. But I know that somebody thought it must be a good idea, I know it is constitutional, and I have no objection to it. But if it is going to impede the passage of the legislation basically, I would be glad to suggest that it be removed.

A few minutes later, Democratic Rep. Forrester of Georgia, pursuing the same line of questioning, asked for clarification about what the attorney general was recommending:

Attorney General Kennedy. Yes; in the original legislation we recommend Federal legislation.

Mr. Forrester. Let me ask you this. What about next year, would you recommend the [same] next year, or do you intend to recommend next year that this law cover State and local elections as was set out in this subcommittee report?

Attorney General Kennedy. I think I covered that in my statement, and I think also in my answers to Congressman Willis. I think that if the Committee decides that they want to cover both Federal and State elections, that it will be satisfactory. In my judgment, based on what we found as a problem, we don't think it is necessary. But if the committee decides that they would like to cover it, then it would certainly be acceptable to us. We think it is constitutional.

Mr. Forrester. Would you of your own initiative, or would the Administration next year recommend legislation covering State elections, local elections, and so forth?

Attorney General Kennedy. You mean if this legislation is passed dealing with Federal elections will we make a recommendation dealing with State elections next?

Mr. Forrester. Yes.

Attorney General Kennedy. No.

But under questioning from Rep. Corman, Democrat of California and a strong supporter of including state elections, Kennedy backed away from what he had just said to Forrester about the need to come back at a later date for legislation to cover state elections.

> **Mr. Corman.** We talked a moment ago about the possibility that if this year we adopted legislation relating to Federal elections only, what might we do in a year or two or three.

> **Attorney General Kennedy.** No, he asked me if I were going to offer some legislation next year.

> **Mr. Corman.** Yes. I would like to inquire, if we should pass this legislation which gives some remedies to people so that they can vote in Federal elections only, and in 2 or 3 years only we found that substantial numbers of people had been found by the Federal courts qualified to vote in Federal elections but were being denied the right to vote in local and State elections, would you agree that that might be a proper concern for the Congress?

> **Attorney General Kennedy.** Yes. The Congressman asked me about next year. I wouldn't think that by next year we would have had the time or opportunity to examine the effect of this legislation. We think the effect of this legislation would be that you could vote both Federal and local. We could be wrong about that. I don't think we would learn in a period of 12 [months], but if we were wrong about it, I would have no hesitancy about coming back and asking for [further] legislation.

Later, Rep. Libonati, the author of the amendment, held the floor with a rambling narrative:

> **Mr. Libonati.** Now, with respect to the first provision, you stated that if there were any need for the State or local governments to receive corrective legislation, to bring about the ultimate goals that are set out in the specific intent of that provision, that you would ask for that in the future; that you were satisfied in limiting the bill to the Federal program. . . .
>
> **Attorney General Kennedy.** Yes, sir.

When Libonati completed his remarks, which had been broken only by an occasional "Yes, sir" from the attorney general, Rep. Kastenmeier of Wisconsin, the strongest supporter of the subcommittee bill, questioned the attorney general:

> **Mr. Kastenmeier.** I do not understand how you can feel that it is not necessary to have State elections in the bill. . . .
>
> **Attorney General Kennedy.** Well, I think I made my position clear. First, Congressman, I have no objection to having the State and Federal in. In my judgment, as a practical matter, Congressman, if you have Federal elections in, it is going to require—it is going to be virtually impossible as a practical matter to set up one booth for State elections and one booth for Federal

elections in connection with registering to vote. I think that is a virtual impossibility. So therefore, I think if you cover Federal elections you will, as a practical matter, cover State elections as well.

The second point that I would make is that there is some feeling by some—now, I do not know what the numbers are, but there is some feeling by some that they would support Federal elections, but they would not support State elections. That might not be just here in the House of Representatives, but it is in the Senate as well.

I think that the vote on this bill is going to be very close. So therefore all I say is that if we can include Federal and State elections, get the bill by on a bipartisan way, that it would be supported—this kind of effort would be supported by both Republicans and Democrats, and that it would not cause any difficulty or put the bill in jeopardy—then I think it should be included. If it is not included I do not think it is a catastrophe, because I think as a practical matter the result would be very much the same. But as it was set up here, if we find after a year or so we are not able to work these things out, perhaps we would have to come back.

Mr. Kastenmeier. I wish I could believe, as you believe, that there would not be a dual system. . . .

Attorney General Kennedy. Congressman, if we can get it by—if I were on this committee, I would support your position on that. I think that is the safest and the best way to proceed. I would hope that it was included. I just raise the question—I do not want to lose support for the bill based on that. But I would support your position if I was on this committee.

Then Chairman Celler broke the tension with a story:

I was in my temple one Sabbath, and the good rabbi of our temple said he was going to tell us about the prophets of the Bible. He spent about an hour on Amos, another hour on Josiah, another hour on Isaiah, one more hour on Zachariah, another hour on Micah. And then he lit up and said, "Now I come to Malachi. What place shall I give Malachi?" And somebody in the rear of the temple said, "Give him my place—I'm tired."

One suspects that the man in the rear of the temple was not the only one who was tired.

The attorney general and the members of the Judiciary Committee had endured an arduous, two-day ordeal. Kennedy had been put through a long, intense interrogation on the bill, with most of the questions centered on parts of the legislation other than the Libonati amendment. But among members of the subcommittee, attention remained focused on Title I and the amendment.

Attorney General Kennedy, however, failed to make a clear statement on the Libonati amendment, saying effectively, *I don't think it is necessary, but I have no objection to it.*

To Representatives Willis, Forrester, and Libonati, he conveyed the impression that he favored limiting voting rights to federal elections alone. He told Forrester that if the bill passed with federal elections covered only, he would not simply turn around and make a recommendation dealing with state elections in the year to come. Yet to Representative Rogers, and especially to Representative Kastenmeier, he clearly indicated that he approved of the subcommittee's change broadening coverage to include state as well as federal elections, taking the position that "we would have to come back" if a similar application to state elections did not work out over the subsequent year. He also made a similar declaration to Representative Corman.

All in all, it did not seem likely that Kennedy had changed any votes.

*   *   *

The probing by the Judiciary Committee Democrats, who raised the question of including both state and federal elections, reflected the differences within the Democratic ranks.

Republicans privately indicated their support of the Libonati amendment. With the possible exception of liberal Republicans Lindsay and Cahill, they would vote for it if it received the backing of the administration and the committee Democrats who favored civil rights legislation. Publicly, however, the Republicans had declared they would make no statements on the question until Chairman Celler and the attorney general made clear their support of the amendment, if in fact they were supporting it.

Neither had done so.

For this reason, Republicans were convinced that Rep. Libonati was being used as a decoy or pinch hitter for the southerners in an effort to lure the Republicans into voting for the amendment, while all northern Democrats except Libonati would be free to oppose the amendment. Until the committee Republicans were convinced otherwise, they would remain silent on the amendment.

The failure of Attorney General Kennedy and Chairman Celler to take a strong position in support of the Libonati amendment seemed like a small thing compared with the great issues of public accommodations and the Federal Employment Practices Commission. Yet it was the pending business before the Judiciary Committee and would be the first matter voted on when the committee resumed its consideration of the bill. Thus, in the struggle to mold a durable, bipartisan coalition in support of the bill, the amendment was of far greater tactical significance than those weightier, more substantive issues.

The way forward was unclear. Democratic members sought guidance from the administration on what to do about this first weakening amendment pending before the committee, but the administration's advice was confusing. If the amendment had been offered by Rep. Willis of Louisiana, their task would have been simple: They would oppose it, and the committee would defeat it overwhelmingly. But the amendment had been offered by Rep. Libonati of Illinois, a civil rights supporter. This made all the difference.

Celler further weakened potential support for a compromise by the way he conducted the hearings. Unfortunately, he allowed the questioning of Attorney General Kennedy to be conducted in a disorganized, haphazard, almost anarchic fashion. There was no order or structure to the way the questions were propounded. As I saw it, he should have taken up the bill title by title and section by section, so that Kennedy and his colleagues could focus their attention on one subject or group of subjects at a time. To do otherwise was unfair to the attorney general. A logical, sequential approach would have tightened consideration of the measure.

I felt Chairman Celler should have insisted that the members restrict their questions to one title at a time. Then, too, there should have been a regular order to the questions by seniority, alternating from one party to the other. In fact, any structured method would have been better than what Celler permitted.

I also thought that Celler erred in not saying firmly and specifically that he supported the Libonati amendment. Why didn't he take a clear stand, and do so right off the bat? Why didn't he ask the attorney general or his colleagues to do likewise? Perhaps the vagueness expressed by the committee reinforced Kennedy's own confusion on the subject.

At one point, Rep. Libonati interjected, "Mr. Chairman, what is this, a private conversation? I mean, after all, this is my amendment here." The members laughed, but it was no laughing matter.

Further confusing things was the fact that committee members were being told to choose between the administration's bill and the subcommittee's. Was there no other alternative? Couldn't the full committee—a group of lawyers, after all—work its will on the bill, title by title and line by line? Clearly, that was one of their functions as legislators.

Public opinion wasn't involved here either, as the Libonati amendment seemed to be a well-kept secret. Had any newspapers even mentioned it? Actually, Peter Kumpa in the *Baltimore Sun* and Richard Lyons in the *Washington Post* did. The *New York Times* hadn't, obviously, because the attorney general didn't want to take a position on it and probably wished the whole thing would go away. Neither Anthony Lewis for the *Times* nor the attorney general had even acknowledged the amendment by name—but then again, no one else did either, except Rep. Libonati. None of the liberal Democrats wanted to get anywhere near it.

Chairman Celler, above all, seemed at sea. He bounced back and forth between committing himself to the subcommittee version and pledging his loyalty to the president. As overseer and architect of the pell-mell, post-tax-cut vote stampede in the subcommittee, Celler had the power and impregnable position to offer the modifying amendments himself. Yet what did he do? He didn't consult any Republicans except McCulloch. Then he abandoned the subcommittee bill and returned to the administration's June proposal.

Obviously, bipartisanship was nothing more than lip service. Who really wanted it? Not the Democrats. And aside from McCulloch and Halleck, not the Republicans either.

We still didn't have bona fide negotiations on a bipartisan bill. Both the Katzenbach–McCulloch and the

Lindsay–Bolling efforts were in limbo. And now we had the attorney general's approach to the Libonati amendment: *I wouldn't vote for it myself, but if it helps us win votes for the president's bill, I'm for it.* The Judiciary Committee chairman's humor, at least, did not desert him. As I recall, when asked whether he personally would introduce the amendments to modify the pending legislation, Celler said: "There's an old Turkish saying that you only roll up your pants when you approach the side of the river."

CHAPTER 8

Who Gets the Credit?
Who Gets the Blame?
October 17–21, 1963

Early on October 17, I learned that Chairman Celler had canceled the Judiciary Committee meeting scheduled for that day. He offered no explanation for the move, but apparently the committee's northern Democrats were not ready publicly to endorse the Libonati amendment. In fact, they were divided on whether to support it at all. The next committee meeting was scheduled for October 22.

In place of the meeting, Attorney General Kennedy, his deputies Nicholas Katzenbach and Burke Marshall, and White House Congressional Relations Chief Larry O'Brien met that morning with the northern Democrats of the

Judiciary Committee. I heard that in a general discussion of the bill's provisions, some of the committee members seemed willing to support the White House–directed move to restrict the bill, while others, led by Rep. Corman and Rep. Kastenmeier, indicated their intent to stick with the broader subcommittee version.

Meanwhile, the action had shifted to the floor of the Senate and House both. In the upper house, Senator Javits of New York warned his fellow Republicans to speak out forcefully against the myth that the bill had to be cut back in order to gain Republican votes.

House Republicans did speak out. Liberal Democrats had taken a one-hour special order in the House to discuss civil rights. A number of Republicans remained on the House floor but made no effort to participate—until Representative Thomas Gill, Democrat of Hawaii, included the following statement in his remarks:

> The reasonably strong and effective civil rights bill approved by the Judiciary subcommittee is now reported to be in the process of compromise, or in a less complimentary phrase, cut back to a form satisfactory to the Republican leadership. Reportedly the cutback is necessary to ensure passage, and the slings and arrows for this move are being accepted generously by the Attorney General.

Minutes later the following exchange occurred between Representative Gill and Representative Charles Teague, Republican of California:

Mr. Teague. I want to ask a question of the gentleman from Hawaii. I was under the impression that I had read in the morning press that the so-called retreat by the Committee on the Judiciary from a stronger civil rights bill was made at the request of Attorney General Mr. Robert Kennedy rather than the members on the committee. Is that correct or incorrect?

Mr. Gill. I believe I mentioned that the Attorney General has decided to take the credit for such a retreat, if indeed there was one, and it was so stated in the paper and was so stated in my remarks.

After a fiery exchange between Rep. Gill and Rep. H. R. Gross, the Republican gadfly from Iowa, Rep. Lindsay sought recognition:

Mr. Lindsay. Mr. Speaker, as the gentleman knows, I am a member of the Committee on the Judiciary which has been studying the subject of a civil rights bill for some time. I do not know whether the press, on this whole subject, has been fair to the people or not; I really do not know. I do know that the press has reported continuously that the reason it is now being suggested that the civil rights bill be cut back in the full Judiciary Committee is in order to get Republican votes. I think that if the administration has made that statement, it is an unfair statement. But I am not sure that the administration has ever said that. I think the press is reading into it a good deal, because the fact of the matter is that it just is not so. You do not have to cut back the bill in order to get Republican votes, because Republicans on the Judiciary Committee will vote for the bill as reported out of the subcommittee.

The colloquy continued with Representative Donald Fraser, Democrat of Minnesota:

> **Mr. Fraser.** Mr. Speaker, I am particularly pleased that the gentleman from New York should announce today—and this is the first time I had heard of it—that all of the Republican members on the House Judiciary Committee are prepared to vote for the civil rights bill as originally reported by the subcommittee. . . .
>
> **Mr. Lindsay.** I am glad that the gentleman has raised that point again, because it does have to be clarified. If any bill is going to be substantially cut back in the full committee, it will be on the motion of the majority side, because they want it that way. The majority of the Republicans, which is all you need to get the bill reported out in its present form—will be happy to support the bill with the present provisions contained in it, subject to possible language modifications and a tightening of the bill. But insofar as the major provisions are concerned such as voting rights and FEPC, the majority of the Republican Members will support them and vote them out, provided the Democratic majority side of the aisle does not take the initiative to cut them back, because they control the show in that committee.
>
> Mr. Speaker, I am delighted that the gentleman raised the point, because I think the press has tended to

play it the other way in indicating that the Republicans were the ones who were initiating proposed changes in these particular items. . . .

I am delighted that I happened to be on the floor this afternoon to hear the discussion, but it just so happens that you do have present on the floor today on the Republican side the gentleman from Minnesota [Mr. MacGregor] and myself. Here are two of us who are going to vote for FEPC and will attempt to hold it in the bill, and we hope there is no effort made to cut it out.

Lindsay had stated, quite clearly, the position of the majority of the Judiciary Committee's Republicans: They would support the subcommittee bill unless and until the committee's northern Democrats initiated efforts to modify the measure. The Republicans would not take the lead in pressing for changes in the legislation.

I had lunch that day with Stuart Rothman, former general counsel to the National Labor Relations Board (NLRB), where we had a fruitful talk on the Federal Employment Practices Commission and possible GOP alternatives and on NLRB race-related cases. I also spoke to John Beckler of the Associated Press, Catherine Mackin of the Hearst Headline Service, and to my surprise, Anthony Lewis of the *New York Times*.

Apparently, Lewis had spoken to Rep. Lindsay, who told him the majority of the Judiciary Republicans were committed to the subcommittee bill. Lewis, however, didn't believe Lindsay, and was talking to me at Rep. McCulloch's suggestion.

"Lindsay is right," I told Lewis. "The majority supports the bill." The NAACP's Clarence Mitchell had told him the same thing.

Yet Lewis remained skeptical, even after I assured him that—to the best of my knowledge and that of others close to the bill—I was not misleading him. "That doesn't go along with what I'm hearing," he replied.

I met with McCulloch in his office the following afternoon, October 18, for a lengthy exchange of views over more than two hours. He had spent the previous morning in a long exploratory meeting with Chairman Celler, where they had covered general ground but reached no agreement on how they might put together a bipartisan compromise. McCulloch and I now analyzed the conflicting strategies surrounding the bill and renewed the search for a way to achieve bipartisan agreement.

With few exceptions, Rep. McCulloch's Republican colleagues on the committee would never accept the administration bill—and I told him that. They had pride in the Republican proposals of January 31 and June 3, and in the work of their counterparts on the Education and Labor Committee regarding the FEPC measure. They wished to incorporate as much of their own handiwork as possible into a bipartisan bill.

For Republicans to bow to the Kennedy administration's demands would be putting a bipartisan label on a Democratic product. It would be an administration bill and an administration triumph. "Sure, they carry on to beat the band about how no civil rights bill can be passed without Republican votes," I told McCulloch. "The fact is, they want all the credit for anything that is favorably received, and they want to pin all the blame on us for anything that fails to happen or is 'unpopular.'

"Congressman McCulloch, if you embrace the administration bill as a compromise, every Republican who worked to create the legislation of January and June; every Republican who testified before the committee; every Republican who has pride of authorship in legislation that represented the fairness, decency, and good will of conscientious members of Congress, would be disturbed—and justifiably so. They will accuse you and Charlie Halleck of going through the White House Rose Garden unnecessarily."

McCulloch listened attentively, and I went on.

"Republicans see no reason to support the Democrats at this time, because they will gain nothing for whatever they do to aid the legislation; because there is no necessity to capitulate to the administration; and because they fear the administration and Celler will refuse to negotiate in good faith. If the Democrats do reach agreement with us in the end, they will renege on the promises they made. The only hope for Republicans is to negotiate from strength: to make it clear that sharing the responsibility for producing a bipartisan measure would bind the administration and committee Democrats to recognize and publicly proclaim the Republicans as equal authors of whatever measure might be turned out. It must be bipartisan in substance as well as in name.

"The Republican members *do* want a more moderate bill than the measure voted out by the subcommittee. But they will never give blanket acceptance to the administration measure when so many of them struggled to fashion legislation while the administration was holding back on the introduction of a bill. Sir, they will never go along with an agreement to accept the administration bill as a compromise. For the majority of House Republicans, that would be a sellout."

McCulloch's reply was equally impassioned. "Bob, the subcommittee bill cannot pass the House. The bill is too strong. We must soften its harsher edges. Our responsibility must be to our country first in this important area. Our party, much as we love her, must occupy the second place here. Who receives credit or blame is of lesser importance. Our main concern is to write a bill that can receive the support of all Americans. Pride of authorship is not so important that we allow a harsh measure to pass which will lead to difficult times and the possibility of blood in the streets.

"This may not be the popular or political thing to do," he continued, "but I assure you it is the right thing. When I was minority leader in the Ohio House of Representatives back in 1936, and our party had only 29 members—and later, when John Bricker was governor and Bob Taft, young Bob's father, was in the Senate, and I was Speaker of the Ohio House of Representatives—we had to make difficult, often unpopular decisions, like the levying of emergency revenue measures. We had to think of the unemployed, the young people who were unable to get work. The good people of our beloved state had to make sacrifices in those difficult days.

"What the press writes and what the opposition says or claims are secondary. We must do what is right. You are young. When you are older, you will not allow yourself to be quite so angry at the imperfections of life and the unfairness of things."

I admired McCulloch's candor, and his willingness to make tough and unpopular decisions no matter how rough the press and the public might be on him. I admired his determination to put country before party. And while I knew my view—to hold the line until we had a truly bipartisan effort—was shared by most Republicans at that time, I realized his was the broader view. Solving a great national crisis was of paramount importance and took precedence over everything—even if it meant letting go of party politics. And although many of the Republicans' worst fears were borne out in the end, McCulloch was proved correct.

* * *

When I arrived at my office the next day, a Saturday, I found a large envelope bearing the stamp COMPLIMENTS OF THE FOURTH DISTRICT OF OHIO. Inside were newspaper articles favorable to McCulloch's position, including a story by Richard Lyons in the *Washington Post*, and an editorial from the *Christian Science Monitor*. Other people on the Hill also received clippings from McCulloch as he worked through the weekend to nail down Republican support for the Libonati amendment.

Monday, October 21, was a day of frenetic activity. At noon, Rep. Lindsay, Rep. Cahill, and Rep. Jim Bromwell of Iowa were the only House Republicans definitely holding out against the move to round up support for Libonati's amendment.

The Justice Department was all over the Hill, trying to win support for the amendment from recalcitrant Democrats. But the civil rights groups were busy too. In midafternoon, David Cohen of the ADA told me that "Libby might withdraw." A few minutes later, Arnie Sawislak of UPI called; he had just left Rep. Libonati's office with the distinct impression that the Democrat from Illinois was pretty disgusted with both the administration and Chairman Celler. According to Sawislak, Libonati said that they weren't supporting him and that he was planning to withdraw the amendment.

I raced to McCulloch's office. It was about 4:30 in the afternoon.

"Bob, what do you know?" he queried.

I replied that from all the indications I had, the Libonati amendment would probably carry if it were put to a vote as expected the following day.

McCulloch seemed pleased with this intelligence. But there was more.

"I have received reliable information that Libonati is planning to withdraw his amendment," I informed him.

As I was relaying this news to McCulloch, his telephone rang. Vera Page, his administrative assistant, said it was the attorney general, calling to ask McCulloch how things looked.

Rep. McCulloch told Attorney General Kennedy he was mildly optimistic that the amendment would be agreed to if Democrats supported it in the same proportion that Republicans would. But he was worried by some disturbing information he had just received—that Rep. Libonati was planning to withdraw his amendment.

The attorney general seemed not to believe him. McCulloch repeated the information, with an admonition that Kennedy ought to look into it. Once the conversation had ended, McCulloch told me that the attorney general had indicated he would check out the report and take whatever steps were required.

As I turned to leave his office, McCulloch called me back.

"Bob," he said, "matters are getting more complex than even you and I were aware of a few days ago. The information you have just brought me is typical of what is happening." In all his 32 years in elected office, he couldn't remember such maneuvering on so important an issue.

CHAPTER 9

"The Situation Was Intolerable"
October 22, 1963

On October 22, the Judiciary Committee convened for its first meeting since the appearance of the attorney general on October 15–16, and its first business session since Representatives Libonati and Tuck had offered their amendments on October 10. What happened, as told to me by Copenhaver, was difficult to believe.

Immediately after the meeting began, Libonati sought recognition by the chair. He demanded that he be allowed to withdraw his amendment. Objections were heard, but Libonati vigorously asserted his right to withdraw. There was nothing in the House Rules, he said, that required him to have unanimous consent before such a request could be honored.

As he wished, the amendment was withdrawn.

Then Rep. Tuck withdrew his amendment.

This move confirmed the suspicions of many Republicans—that Tuck's amendment had been used to suggest the existence of a separate southern Democratic position.

GOP Representative Meader of Michigan then offered an amendment to Title I, to establish a commission that would examine the possibility of enforcing section 2 of the 14th Amendment. Section 2 called for a reduction in congressional representation for those states that did not comply with the 14th Amendment. As the committee began to discuss Meader's amendment, Representative Robert Ashmore, Democrat of South Carolina, offered a motion to recommit the bill to the subcommittee. A roll call was taken, and the motion failed 9–21. Meader's amendment was then defeated by a voice vote.

At 11:55 a.m., Chairman Celler recognized Representative Arch Moore, Republican of West Virginia, recently returned from Geneva. Rep. Moore, to the astonishment of almost everyone in the room, offered a motion to report the subcommittee bill from the full committee without change. The motion was quickly seconded by Rep. Rogers of Colorado, a Democrat—an action that made the move bipartisan. A vote was ordered, shutting off debate.

The clerk was directed to call the roll. As the roll call began, the noon bell rang. The House was now in session.

Under the House rules, a committee (with certain privileged exceptions) could not meet when the House was in session, without the unanimous consent of the House. Thus, an objection was made to completing the roll call.

As Chairman Celler gaveled the meeting to a close, pandemonium reigned. If time had allowed the completion of the roll call, the Moore motion would have prevailed. The subcommittee bill would have been released to the Rules Committee and the floor of the House—to what would have been, at best, an uncertain fate.

Members later described the mood of the committee that day, even before the Moore motion, as "utter chaos." The Judiciary Committee was in so sorry a state that it could not legislate. It was felt that further deliberations on the bill at that time would only compound the confusion and end as an exercise in futility. Moore's motion seemed the quickest way out of a hopeless impasse: Committee Democrats were totally unwilling to undo the handiwork of the subcommittee for which they had been responsible, and the Republicans were not prepared to let them off the hook.

With pressure from the civil rights groups as great as it was, neither the Republicans nor the Democrats dared assume the dangerous political risks involved in initiating the move for a milder bill.

The Democrats now faced the likelihood that the Moore motion to report out the subcommittee's civil rights bill would be overwhelmingly approved at the committee's next meeting, and the Democrats' expansive bill would almost certainly suffer on the House floor. Or they could negotiate in good faith to arrive at a bipartisan bill.

The "generals"—Celler and McCulloch—were having a rough day. Chairman Celler's strategy to put the Democrats on top had, conversely, come down on top of him. And Rep. McCulloch was taking a beating from an unlikely quarter—the Department of Justice.

At first, the Kennedy administration was merely crestfallen; then, they became genuinely angry and accused the Republicans of bad faith. When McCulloch reminded Deputy Attorney General Katzenbach and Assistant Attorney General Marshall of what he had told the attorney general the previous afternoon—that Libonati might withdraw his amendment—the two men denied having been informed of this. Twice during the afternoon of October 22, McCulloch phoned and asked me to repeat what I had heard him say to the attorney general over the phone. I did, but he still wasn't satisfied.

So he called me to his office, where we went over it again. He said that the attorney general had at first denied being forewarned about Libonati's intentions, but after McCulloch explained that he could produce a witness to the call, Attorney General Kennedy recalled having been told and asking Assistant AG Marshall to take care of it. However, McCulloch told me, he had just spoken to Marshall, who said no one had said anything in advance to him about Libonati withdrawing his amendment. I wasn't sure what to believe, but it seemed to me that AG Kennedy wasn't being entirely upfront.

McCulloch then added that he had "had words" with the attorney general. "Something has to be done about this," he continued. "Maybe I have been too trusting. So many of my colleagues have warned me. You know, I should have known better when [AG Kennedy] told John Lindsay, in a most arrogant fashion, that he had not had time to read major legislation in the field."

Within minutes, McCulloch telephoned Minority Leader Halleck, and they quickly agreed: Halleck would advise the president that the Republicans would prefer that the attorney general no longer participate in the negotiations on the Hill. Taking care to express that there were no hard feelings against Katzenbach and Marshall, Halleck asked the president to take personal command.

As the afternoon wore on, support mounted for the Moore motion. Ohio's Representative Brown, of the Rules Committee, told Lindsay that at least 10 of the 14 committee Republicans would vote for it. After speaking to Brown, Lindsay called Representative Carlton King, Republican of New York, and learned that King also would support the Moore motion.

A most important day for the civil rights bill was coming to a close. Moore's motion was a bold and brilliant move, surely the turning point in the bill's journey through Congress. It forced the participants to stop fencing with each other and begin talking in good faith—and it would soon bring President Kennedy directly and swiftly into the negotiations.

With motions withdrawn, motions to recommit, and finally a motion to report directly to the House, it seemed that the legislative process was being turned inside out. But if the Judiciary Committee agreed to Moore's motion, debate in the committee would be completely bypassed on the most significant bill to come before it in an entire generation—perhaps even longer. The civil rights bill would head straight to the House floor.

Ironically, that very afternoon, I delivered a speech to a group of cadets from the Africa Officers Corps on the civil rights bill as an illustration of how a law is made under the US system of government. Perhaps they thought my textbook explanation of how a bill becomes a law was difficult to grasp. In fact, what was happening in the Judiciary Committee at the very moment I was speaking was as far removed from customary legislative process as Nigeria was from our nation's capital.

*   *   *

How did events take such a decisive turn? More precisely, why did Rep. Libonati withdraw his amendment? And why did Rep. Moore offer his motion to consider the subcommittee's strong civil rights legislation?

Chairman Celler had made a huge mistake. His selection of Libonati as a replacement for Willis to offer the initial amendment to modify the subcommittee bill had totally backfired. In the words of *Time* magazine, Celler "picked Libonati partly because of Lib's record of strict party obedience, partly because Lib did not need to worry about political repercussions in his machine-run district." Yet in fact, Celler must have known that Libonati was not a down-the-party-line man, but one of the most independent and colorful figures in the House.

Celler was equally erroneous in thinking that "Lib" had little to worry about in terms of blowback from his district. Although on the surface it was an enclave dominated by the Democratic Party machine under Mayor Richard J. Daley, Libonati's district had a large Black constituency and was at the center of Chicago's civil rights upheaval. Civil rights groups in Chicago were preparing to flood the papers with the news that Libonati was the author of a major amendment to weaken the bill. As an amendment to exempt state and local elections from coverage of the act, it prompted one wag to call it, as I recall, "the Boss Daley amendment," implying that deprivation of an individual's right to vote in an election in Mayor Daley's Chicago would not be covered by the bill.

To compound Libonati's problems, on the day his amendment would have come up for a vote, great numbers of Chicagoans were engaged in the massive Chicago school boycott organized by civil rights groups. Thus, he was hardly an ideal candidate for the role he had been called upon to perform: offering an amendment to weaken the civil rights bill.

But it was Manny Celler himself who delivered the final blow to the Libonati amendment. *Time* magazine offered a humorous account of Libonati's response to Celler's political gyrations:

All might have gone well—if Celler had kept his mouth shut and if Lib were not a televiewer. But Celler submitted to a television interview. Libonati caught the show, and did not like what he heard. Explained Libonati later:

"So then I'm sitting down, just like you and me are sitting here now, and I'm watching television and who do I see on the television but my chairman [Celler]. And he's telling 'em up there in his district that he's for a strong bill, and that he doesn't have anything to do with any motion to cut the bill down. So when I hear that,

I says to myself, 'Lib, where are we at here, anyway?' And I think that if they're gonna get some Republican votes anyway, and if the chairman says he doesn't have anything to do with my motion, then certain representations that were made to me is [sic] out the window. So, I withdraw my motion."

Still, Libonati might have gone along with Celler if he had received support from both his committee chairman and the attorney general. But neither man made forthright statements in support of the amendment. Therefore, Libonati withdrew it.

Unlike Libonati's withdrawal of his amendment, Arch Moore's motion came as a surprise to everyone except two House colleagues. He later described to me his motivation at the time.

Earlier in October, as the subcommittee bill was being considered by the full committee, Rep. Moore had been at the International Committee on European Migration convention in Geneva, Switzerland. While away from Washington, Moore had kept informed of happenings on the civil rights bill by reading the Paris edition of the *New York Herald Tribune*. One afternoon, while sipping drinks with Republican colleagues Rep. MacGregor of Minnesota and Rep. Abner Sibal of Connecticut on the veranda of the Hotel du Rhône, he had an idea.

From the *Trib*, he knew of the maneuvering that was going on over the legislation. So he told Sibal and MacGregor that after returning to Washington, he would let "the farce" go on for another week. "If nothing happens by then, I'm going to move to report out the subcommittee bill and call the Democrats' bluff," he insisted.

"I'm not a rubber-stamp congressman," Moore explained to me. "I know my people sent me here to do things. I'm always trying to think of the best way of accomplishing what matters to me. I saw pretty quickly that the shortest way to bring order out of the chaos in the committee, and get everybody off the hook at the same time, would be to make the motion to report the subcommittee bill. The situation was intolerable."

Moore said he knew legislation in the area of civil rights was a must. "It was absolutely necessary," he continued. "I knew there would be a conflagration if there were no bill. I wanted to see the deadlock broken and wanted to put the responsibility right where it belonged. My motion to report was the quickest way to accomplish that end."

But outside of MacGregor and Sibal, nobody knew what he was up to.

"McCulloch didn't know what I was going to do until maybe ten seconds before I made the motion," Moore acknowledged. "He wasn't very happy, I must say. But there wasn't a damn thing he could do about it. You know, it made a hero out of him. Halleck, too."

If the roll call had been completed at that time, Moore told me, there would have been at least 10 votes to report the bill. But Celler and McCulloch had been playing with the bill for weeks, and they were nowhere. Everybody, from the press to the administration, went to them to find out what was happening. The experts all figured that whatever Celler and McCulloch would do, their junior colleagues would also do.

"How wrong could people be?" Moore wondered. "If I ever saw two generals without troops, they were Celler and McCulloch. They were so busy making deals between themselves without consulting their colleagues in advance that they were out of touch with sentiment in the House. They were so used to being statesmen, they forgot that most of us are ordinary political animals. On that day, the troops were so far out ahead of the generals, it was hard to believe."

The next several days were a time of conferences—of backtracking and trying to see a way forward. The Capitol was a beehive of activity. In fact, as I attempt to recapture the most eventful week in that eventful month of drama and confusion, I find it difficult to recall a moment when there wasn't a critical meeting concerning the fate of the civil rights bill.

And there was no time to waste.

CHAPTER 10

The President Intervenes
October 23–24, 1963

Supporters of the Moore motion—to present the Democratic subcommittee bill directly to the House without debate or amendments in the full Judiciary Committee—had difficulty defending their position. Both the Kennedy administration and the press were heavily arrayed against them. Without further consideration in Subcommittee No. 5—not only of Title I and public accommodations, but of the entire bill— the legislation would likely face strong opposition in the House from southern Democrats and conservative Republicans alike, and would risk being drastically weakened. But this legislation was far too important to let it die without making sure it first had a fighting chance.

Speaking on the *Today* show, Rep. John Lindsay stated the problem succinctly: Even if the administration suddenly came out for "separate but equal," the press would support it. His point was that anything the administration did was right, while everything the Republicans did was wrong or obstructionist unless it had the support of the administration. The touchstone of proper behavior, it seemed, was support of the administration.

Not surprisingly, the committee meeting on October 23 was canceled as the Department of Justice struggled to stem the tide for the Moore motion, a cause that grew more desperate as the powerful Leadership Conference on Civil Rights brought its full weight into the fray at its usual Wednesday afternoon meeting.

I joined the civil rights workers, labor officials, church representatives, and members of allied and kindred organizations who were packed to overflowing that day in the Leadership Conference's cramped quarters on the seventh floor of the Mills Building on Pennsylvania Avenue. Clarence Mitchell of the NAACP presided, flanked by Joseph Rauh and Arnold Aronson, secretary of the Leadership Conference.

Mitchell made a few introductory remarks on the exciting new development—the Moore motion. Then Andrew Biemiller, chief lobbyist for the AFL-CIO, spoke forcefully of the need to get Republican votes for the Moore motion and of the difficulty of ever being sure what Republicans were likely to do. Biemiller's sentiments were echoed by other union leaders present. To my surprise, the meeting already had become quite partisan.

Mitchell then called on me, as a Republican staffer, to say a few words about the attitude of the Republicans toward the Moore motion. I told the assemblage that at least eight and possibly 11 of the 14 committee Republicans (out of 35 total committee members) were prepared to vote for the Moore motion.

I then addressed my remarks to Biemiller. I told him to be fair, for Republicans were as committed to civil rights legislation as Democrats were. I said it was wrong to treat the Republican position on civil rights as if it were a minimum-wage question.

Reporting on the Democrats were Mitchell and Rauh; Bill Higgs, the Washington representative of the Student Nonviolent Coordinating Committee; and David Cohen of Americans for Democratic Action. After further discussion, there was a pause. Suddenly, spirits seemed to rise; smiles brightened, and enthusiasm for the task at hand became contagious, embracing nearly everyone in the room. It was assignment time—time to line up the organizations to call on the Judiciary Committee members and urge them to support the Moore motion.

Rauh began to call the roll of the committee members. "Emanuel Celler, Democrat, Brooklyn, New York. Who's going to visit him?"

Representatives of various organizations responded: "ADA" and "American Jewish Committee" and "Anti-Defamation League" were heard through the din as members of the Leadership Conference pledged their group to talk to Celler.

Rauh continued reading the list, and groups that were

especially strong in a committee member's district volunteered to talk to that member. As each member's name was called, a cacophony of voices could be heard.

"Steelworkers!"

"National Council of Churches!"

"ACLU!"

Now and again during the litany, the deep voice of Biemiller could be heard interjecting, "The AFL-CIO of Newark, New Jersey . . . Cedar Rapids, Iowa . . . Worcester, Massachusetts."

Rauh prefaced the "bidding" with a short sketch of each member: how he had voted in the past, how he was likely to vote now. When he came to Rep. McCulloch, Rauh acknowledged that the congressman had been remarkably unwavering, but said, "We mustn't let up. How about it?"

"Put the churches on him," someone said after a pause.

"Yeah, that's it," said someone else.

"AFL-CIO of Piqua, Ohio," Biemiller thundered, and on it went, for McCulloch and the rest of the committee.

"SNCC!"

"Meat Cutters!"

"ILGWU!"

"Friends Committee!"

"Jewish War Veterans!"

"National Catholic Conference!"

"IUE!"

"UAW!"

"Amalgamated Clothing Workers!"

THE PRESIDENT INTERVENES   131

"Clarence will personally see everybody."

"And the AFL-CIO of Beaumont, Texas . . . Wichita, Kansas . . . Wheeling, West Virginia . . ."

"Hey, that's Arch Moore's district."

"Hell, I've known a lot of fellows who haven't voted for their own motions."

I rode back to the Hill that day with Evelyn Dubrow of the International Ladies Garment Workers Union (ILGWU), who later called to tell me that Democrats Donahue (of Massachusetts) and Libonati were "solid," and that a telegram had been sent to Rep. William St. Onge, Democrat of Connecticut. "We have at least 22 votes," she said.

"Is there a chance the administration can find a way to defeat it?" I asked.

"Not a chance," she said, "unless they come up with a substitute with great appeal, and come up with it fast. After all, Bob, you can't beat something with nothing. At this point, the administration doesn't have anything they can put forward except their old bill, which you Republicans won't support. So there we are." She shrugged her shoulders and smiled, clearly confident in her prediction.

Later that day, President Kennedy intervened directly in the battle.

At about 6:00 p.m., the president summoned six House leaders to the White House: Speaker McCormack, Majority Leader Albert, and Chairman Celler for the Democrats; Minority Leader Halleck, Minority Whip Arends, and Ranking Judiciary Republican McCulloch for the Republicans. With the president were Vice President Lyndon Johnson and Deputy Attorney General Katzenbach representing the Department of Justice. In light of the friction with McCulloch, the attorney general was not included in the meeting. The presence of Vice President Johnson, however, was especially significant; the administration needed his knowledge of how to deal with Congress right now, as they had seldom needed it before.

I heard the details later from Halleck and McCulloch, who said the meeting lasted for about an hour but produced no spectacular results. The only concrete outcome of the session was the president's request that Celler cancel meetings of the committee for the remainder of the week. Celler readily agreed. Those present concurred that there was no hope of heading off the Moore motion unless a substitute could be put forward that would attract sufficient bipartisan support to clear the Judiciary. Everyone committed to working toward that end.

President Kennedy said he would pursue the prospect of a substitute bill at a meeting he was scheduling the next morning with committee Democrats. Halleck and McCulloch told the president they would explore the possibility of a substitute with the committee's Republicans, but could promise no concrete results. Every time they had tried to reach an agreement with the administration on a moderate measure, they explained, they had been blasted by the GOP's rank and file. Partisan feeling remained high.

Halleck said, "Our boys aren't going to be anxious to help out unless you can persuade the Democrats to take the lead."

"The country needs legislation," President Kennedy said, adding that he would do his best, and that both parties would lose if this continued to be a partisan issue. "We all have to assume responsibility to see that a bill passes."

The president directed Deputy AG Katzenbach to keep the lines open with the Republicans at all times, and to do everything possible to produce a compromise by the weekend—one that would be acceptable to committee members of both parties and to the administration. This, Kennedy pointed out, was especially important since southerners of both parties appeared to be planning to support the bill when the Moore motion came to a vote.

True to his word, the president invited the committee's northern Democrats to a morning White House session the next day, October 24. According to what I heard, he stressed the importance of reaching an agreement on the bill, but said he would not pressure them. He emphasized his unhappiness with a provision in Title I, and indicated that he opposed the census proposal on registration and voting statistics because of the cost. Many of the members present told him that in the absence of a satisfactory alternative, they would stick with the subcommittee bill.

That same morning, from 10:30 a.m. until noon, Celler, McCulloch, and Katzenbach renewed their discussions, with Republican Rep. Meader and committee counsels Bill

Foley and Bill Copenhaver also present. Although the meeting resolved a few minor points, it failed to bring about an agreement on a satisfactory alternative to the subcommittee bill.

Minority Leader Halleck expressed his views at a joint morning news conference with Senate Minority Leader Everett Dirksen of Illinois (the "Ev and Charlie show," as everybody referred to their joint appearances) after a meeting of the Senate–House Leadership Conference. Speaking to reporters, Halleck said that things were written into the bill before it came to the committee that would be very difficult for him to support, and that he would continue to try to draft something that could become law.

The day's most important meeting, however, involved the Republican leadership and the House Judiciary Committee Republicans. From 12:30 p.m. until almost 3:00 p.m., they gathered in their customary meeting spot—the whip's office in the Capitol. Halleck and McCulloch told me that, as before, they urged their GOP colleagues to cooperate with the administration in an effort to break the deadlock.

Almost everyone else present differed to some degree regarding their position. Rep. Moore indicated that he would not withdraw his motion under any circumstance. Rep. Brown of Ohio declared his support for the Moore motion and urged McCulloch and Halleck to be a lot tougher in their negotiations with the administration. Halleck summed up Brown's admonition: "If you boys don't think they'll con you, you have another thing coming. If they don't go back on their word now, they're sure as hell to later. They're so desperate now, they might promise anything."

Rep. Brown went on to stress the importance of exploring every possibility, on the slim chance they could reach an agreement that the committee's Republicans could support. Rep. Byrnes, chairman of the House Republican Policy Committee, and Rep. Ford, chairman of the House Republican Conference, called the Moore motion a trump card, indicating that it could force the Kennedy administration into good-faith discussions that heretofore had been lacking in its approach to the problem.

Rep. Arends admonished his colleagues about being overzealous to make the first move. "Let them make the first move," he said. "It's their mess, not ours. They got themselves into it."

McCulloch called me after the big Republican meeting in the whip's office. He asked why the other Republican committee members were so resentful of the approach that he and Halleck were pursuing. I replied that members felt they had been too patient for too long with the committee Democrats and the administration, and that they wanted McCulloch and Halleck to lead the way in fighting for the Republican legislation—or at least for strong Republican input into some kind of compromise.

Rep. Lindsay was so angry with all the maneuvering that he called a press conference to get his position out to the public. He wasn't willing to let his Republicans bear the brunt of the blame if no solution was reached. He thought the press would listen and help propel the process forward.

His anguished remarks, which I made sure to note assiduously, captured the frustration felt so keenly at that time by Republican supporters of civil rights legislation:

> A few days ago the Republican Minority was under attack because it was "watering down" civil rights legislation, and the cry was that there must be a moderate bill that Republicans would support. Now apparently any Republican who supports the subcommittee bill in principle is killing the legislation with kindness. On the other hand, subtract one word from the Administration's bill and it is "watering down"; add one word and it is killing it.
>
> The current line being put out by the Administration is that "we don't know what the Republicans want." Like Alice, I am in Wonderland. Republicans very early introduced legislation that was advanced and far-reaching. The Attorney General went out of his way to say that he didn't even take the time to read this legislation. That legislation is still there, remains offered and also untouched and unread by the very people who suggest that Republicans had offered nothing.

Syndicated columnist Doris Fleeson wrote the only column favorable to the Moore motion. She strongly articulated the exasperation of congressional members who felt they had become actors in a White House–directed scenario. Aside from the Fleeson column and the fair, objective work of Sawislak and Beckler for the wire services, the press was generally presenting the issue in the way they knew the Kennedy administration would like.

The administration was seen as reasonable; the civil rights groups and Republicans, not so.

A day of conferences and activity, October 24, had come to an end. Throughout the day, I had gone from phone calls to meetings in what seemed like a dizzying blur. I spoke with Robert Semple of the *New York Times* and Catherine Mackin; with David Cohen, Bill Higgs, and Arnie Aronson; with Republican Rep. Fred Schwengel and Rep. Bromwell of Iowa; and with the NAACP's Mitchell—twice. The forces supporting the Moore motion were still intact; an estimated 22 to 25 of the 35 committee members favored the motion that would support the strong civil rights legislation as crafted earlier by Chairman Celler and his handpicked members of Subcommittee No. 5.

Some Judiciary Committee members supported the Moore motion because they wanted a very strong civil rights bill. Others, namely the southern Democrats on the committee, were in favor of the motion because they hoped the bill would fail; they weren't going to support any legislation that gave more rights to Blacks, especially since their own districts would bear most of the changes to schools, voting rights, lunch counters, and other corners of everyday life.

The remaining committee members opposed the Moore motion because they knew the subcommittee bill was so pro–civil rights, it would likely fail—and they desperately wanted something that could win enough votes to become law. The Kennedy administration, also fearing the subcommittee bill was too far-reaching, likewise opposed the Moore motion.

At day's end, there was no draft in circulation of a substitute for the subcommittee bill. There was one bill on the table, and only one.

CHAPTER 11

Progress toward a Compromise
October 25–27, 1963

Fridays were normally quiet on the Hill, but October 25, 1963, was an exception. In the morning, Bill Copenhaver came to my Republican Legislative Research Association office, which was in the Hotel Congressional. Looking glum but determined, the minority counsel asked whether anything could be done to mobilize Republican opposition to the Moore motion. I told him I thought it would be a waste of time to even try.

I spoke bluntly. "How can we bail the Democrats out after the way they've treated us? These Republicans are members of Congress and wish to be treated as spokesmen for the people they represent. I think they're pretty tired of being puppets in a dumb show, with the White House and the Department of Justice pulling the strings. We've been through too much with this to save the Democrats now."

"What happens," Copenhaver asked, "when the bill gets to the Rules Committee?"

"They'll send it to the House floor," I said, "where it will either pass or be cut to pieces. Or they'll make a deal to modify it before letting it clear Rules. What difference does it make?"

"The only difference," he replied, "is between a good bill and a sloppy bill."

He quietly reminded me that when we had started this process back in January, we had wanted a comprehensive, bipartisan bill—and that our goal hadn't changed.

"Sure, you're mad. We're all mad, and with reason," Copenhaver continued, "but we've got to do what's right. The Moore motion may have saved the bill, but voting for it—no matter how tempting that is politically—is wrong, because it is a complete evasion of our responsibility to improve the legislation. At any rate, will you talk to John Lindsay? Without him, nothing can be done."

I told him I would speak to my boss, but I thought it would be better if Rep. McCulloch took the initiative. If McCulloch and Lindsay could arrive at an accord, perhaps a bill could be written. Copenhaver and I were well aware that if the two of them were not together on this, there was little hope for civil rights legislation in the first session of the 88th Congress.

Thus, with misgivings, I agreed with Copenhaver: We should make one more try for a bipartisan agreement.

For the 38th time—or was it the 56th? I had lost track!—Copenhaver and I reviewed the pending civil rights legislation. We again considered these questions: What did the Republicans want? What did each member feel about every provision of the subcommittee bill? What simply had to be in a civil rights bill? What administration provisions could all members live with? What was negotiable? What would we refuse to budge on?

What would satisfy the civil rights groups? What would satisfy the NAACP's Clarence Mitchell? SNCC's Bill Higgs?

Could we persuade the Kennedy administration to tighten and clarify the vague, open-ended, ambiguous language that gave the administration broad discretion—the kind of discretion it could use or not use, depending on political considerations or personal whim?

Speaking of the Kennedy administration, would it keep its word? Could President Kennedy influence enough northern Democrats to turn away from the subcommittee bill in order to swing the balance?

What would the southerners do? Would it be to their advantage to support the subcommittee bill by voting for the Moore motion? If there were a substitute, could they taint that new bill by supporting it instead?

Would the Department of Justice accept some kind of Part III and agree to a permanent Civil Rights Commission? How much of the 14th Amendment could be included in the Title II public accommodations language? Would state as well as federal elections be covered? Would it be the referee provision or the three-judge court to determine whether an individual was qualified to vote?

Back in the House, would Halleck and McCulloch accept some kind of FEPC? What kind of vote fraud amendment did Rep. Cramer of Florida want? Would Rep. Moore withdraw his motion? Could McCulloch and Lindsay even reach an agreement?

Above all, we asked ourselves one question: Was it possible to put something together by Tuesday, October 29, the date of the next committee meeting?

* * *

After we finished our review, Copenhaver and I met Catherine Mackin of Hearst Headline Service for lunch in the Senate dining room. Then I talked to Phyllis Piotrow and Milt Eisenberg in Sen. Keating's office and people from Sen. Scott's staff. I went back to my office and spoke by phone with Bill Higgs, David Cohen, and Clarence Mitchell. I also called Eugenia Daugherty in Rep. Cahill's office and Stan Langland in Rep. MacGregor's office, and told them there was still no change to the legislation. It would be the Moore motion unless and until there was an alternative—and so far, there was none.

I had a long phone chat with Joe Loftus of the *New York Times*, who, unlike his colleague Anthony Lewis, seemed objective and did not merely want confirmation of what the attorney general told him. I also spoke to Meg Greenfield of news magazine *The Reporter*, who asked a lot of acute and probing questions, many of which I was unable to answer.

Rep. Lindsay was heading to a relative's wedding in Richmond, Virginia, over the weekend, and was not planning to return to Washington until Sunday noon. He left an address and telephone number at which he could be reached. Before leaving, he continued work on a draft of a revised Title III. Then he attended a meeting with Rep. Bromwell, Republican Rep. Garner Shriver of Kansas, and Rep. MacGregor. They agreed that the next move was up to the administration.

It was late Friday afternoon when I went to Rep. McCulloch's office. He ushered me into his private room, where we reviewed the events of the past week. "Why did Libonati withdraw?" he asked.

I reiterated what I thought was the primary reason: Chairman Celler and Attorney General Kennedy had not given Rep. Libonati assurances of support.

When McCulloch asked where he could reach Lindsay, I gave him the address and phone number in Richmond, not knowing whether he would resort to using it. At that time, he said nothing about his plans. But spread out on his desk was a large sheet of paper listing the names of the Republican Judiciary Committee members and the Republican leadership, and their whereabouts for the weekend.

I knew then he was planning to try to salvage the bill.

As I prepared to call it a day, McCulloch asked me to check in with him on Saturday and Sunday. I told him I would be in the office on both days. He kidded me about my "banker's hours."

"Bob, sometimes I call your office at 8:30 a.m., and there is no one there," he chuckled. "You start work later than I did when I was your age."

"We city boys may start slow at the first glow, but we gather strength as the day wanes," I joked. "When the farm boys have called it a day, we're still at it, keeping watch through the night."

"Well," McCulloch concluded, "if I were as young as you, I'd be keeping watch too. I hope she's pretty."

*　*　*

On October 26, a Saturday, McCulloch worked all day to assemble a "compromise" civil rights bill. Acting on the views of his colleagues and staff as to what might be an acceptable compromise, and relying on his own experienced judgment as to what should be in the bill, he renewed his discussions with Deputy Attorney General Katzenbach and began to touch base with every Republican member of the committee who might be favorable to a civil rights bill.

McCulloch spoke to each member personally or left word for the member to call him back. He spoke to the members of the Republican leadership as well. From everyone he spoke to, he requested advice on disputed provisions and sought their reaction to a tentative substitute bill, which was now beginning to take shape as a result of his talks with Katzenbach.

By Saturday evening, McCulloch had arrived at a preliminary accord with Katzenbach on all but about a dozen outstanding issues. He also had secured tentative backing for many areas of this agreement from the Republicans he had been able to reach during the day. The discussions between McCulloch and Katzenbach revealed a number of unresolved issues.

In Title I, on voting, the administration pressed its original temporary referee provision, while McCulloch continued to push for the three-judge court proposal, which had been rejected in the subcommittee. There was still uncertainty over the subject matter of the Libonati amendment—whether the coverage of Title I should be limited to federal elections (as desired by the administration and many of the Republicans) or include state elections as well (as was provided for in the subcommittee bill and was being urged by the Leadership Conference on Civil Rights, most liberal Democrats, and some Republicans).

McCulloch and Katzenbach revived their agreement of mid-September on public accommodations (Title II), which closely corresponded to the approach outlined by the attorney general in his appearance before the Judiciary Committee on October 15–16. Meanwhile, the Kennedy administration continued to seek the elimination of Title III—the attorney general's power to initiate or intervene in civil suits regarding deprivations of civil rights—from the bill. Although the administration's approach was supported by many Republicans and some Democrats, it was strongly opposed by Lindsay, the Leadership Conference, and many northern Democrats—most notably, the provision's author, Rep. Rogers of Colorado, whose constituent was imprisoned in Americus, Georgia.

There were no major disagreements on the education title (Title IV). But the administration still favored the creation of the Community Relations Service (a particular favorite of Vice President Johnson) within Title V; the Republicans strongly opposed it. Conversely, Republicans were united in their support of a permanent Civil Rights Commission, whereas the administration continued to seek only a four-year extension. Republicans were pressing to broaden the commission's authority to investigate instances of vote fraud. This was opposed by liberal Democrats and the administration.

On Title VI, there now appeared to be basic agreement. The administration had acceded to Rep. Meader's request that the civil injunctive authority be removed. The administration had also honored Rep. McCulloch's wish: The bill's coverage would be limited to grant, interest, and loan provisions, and programs of insurance, guaranty, or otherwise would be eliminated.

Two major questions remained unresolved on the matter of a Federal Employment Practices Commission, within Title VII. First, would there be an FEPC in the bill? Second, if such a provision were included, would the enforcement be by a National Labor Relations Board-type commission or through a civil suit and trial de novo (a new trial) in a federal district court? The administration, the Leadership Conference, and liberals of both parties favored the creation of the commission, which would address discrimination by employers, unions, and the federal government. Traditionally, the Republican leadership had been opposed to an FEPC, disagreeing especially on the enforcement provision. The House Committee on Education and Labor had supported court enforcement in the 87th Congress (through a trial de novo in federal district court) and switched to commission enforcement in the 88th. Support remained for both positions.

For many days, McCulloch had consulted with Representative Robert Griffin of Michigan, the leading Republican spokesman on labor matters in the Education and Labor Committee, and co-author of the Landrum–Griffin Labor Management Reporting and Disclosure Act of 1959. Rep. Griffin favored the creation of an FEPC; his view was shared by a majority of his Republican colleagues on the Education and Labor Committee. Griffin had urged McCulloch to support the committee's position in the 87th Congress, and McCulloch now adopted Griffin's position on court enforcement for the commission.

A dispute over the Title VIII census on registration and voting statistics centered on the administration's contention that the proposal would cost $80 million. The administration wanted to remove the title altogether, but Republicans insisted that it be kept intact. However, the remand provision added in the subcommittee (Title IX) was acceptable to all parties favoring the legislation.

Early Sunday morning, McCulloch was in his office again. Throughout the day, he continued his effort to secure agreement on a compromise bill, sharing developments with Halleck every step of the way throughout the weekend.

At 4:15 p.m. Sunday, Rep. Lindsay arrived at Rep. McCulloch's office wearing Bermuda shorts and tennis shoes—an amusing mismatch with McCulloch's outfit of a blazer, slacks, and a vest. Copenhaver and I were with them, and for two hours we all hashed out the subjects discussed by McCulloch and Katzenbach, reviewing the unresolved issues between them.

PROVISION OF BILL	KENNEDY ADMINISTRATION	MCCULLOCH (R-OH)	LINDSAY (R-NY)	NORTHERN DEMOCRATS	LEADERSHIP CONFERENCE ON CIVIL RIGHTS
TITLE I TEMP. REF. OR 3-JUDGE COURT	Temporary Referees	3-Judge Court	3-Judge Court	*Most:* Temporary Referees *Few:* 3-Judge Court	Same as Northern Democrats
FEDERAL ELECTIONS OR ALL ELECTIONS	Federal Elections	Federal Elections	All Elections	Divided	All Elections
TITLE II PUBLIC ACCOMMODATIONS	Katzenbach–McCulloch Agreement	All Favor Strong Bill with Broad Coverage, Use of 14th Amendment, and Commerce Clause			
TITLE III ATTORNEY GENERAL POWER TO INTERVENE	Opposed	Opposed	In Favor	In Favor	In Favor
TITLE IV EDUCATION	Basic Agreement Among All				
TITLE V COMMUNITY RELATIONS SERVICE	In Favor	Opposed	Opposed	In Favor	In Favor
CIVIL RIGHTS COMMISSION	4-Year Extension	Permanent	Permanent	Permanent	Permanent
VOTE FRAUD	Opposed	In Favor	In Favor	In Favor	In Favor
TECHNICAL ASSISTANCE	In Favor	Opposed	In Favor	In Favor	In Favor
TITLE VI NON-DISCRIMINATION IN FEDERAL PROGRAMS	Katzenbach–McCulloch Agreement Acceptable to All				
TITLE VII FEPC	In Favor	Unknown	In Favor	In Favor	In Favor
FEPC ENFORCEMENT	Commission	Court	Commission	Commission	Commission
TITLE VIII CENSUS TITLE	Opposed	In Favor	In Favor	Indifferent	In Favor
TITLE IX REMAND	All in Favor				

The positions maintained over the weekend of October 26–27 by the various groups favoring civil rights legislation.

On the questions where McCulloch and Lindsay were in accord, they pledged a renewed effort to persuade the Justice Department to accede to Republican demands. As for questions where the two men differed, they agreed that both of them would back McCulloch's Title I limited to federal elections, support a more modest (but still surprisingly strong) accommodations provision, and accept a court-enforced FEPC. On Part III, McCulloch said he would go along with some kind of provision if one were needed to secure agreement on a bill.

When they finally shook hands in agreement, Rep. McCulloch was pleased. Without Rep. Lindsay's support, there could be no hope at all of breaking the impasse. Lindsay, meanwhile, was satisfied that his more moderate colleague was willing to support so strong a bill.

"If you're willing to go this far," Lindsay told McCulloch, "I'm willing to stand by you all the way. But it will be rough. The pressure will be enormous."

Before the meeting concluded, the two representatives asked Copenhaver and me to meet with Katzenbach and Marshall early the next morning, to negotiate on their behalf the remaining items in disagreement—those where McCulloch and Lindsay came down on one side and the administration on the other. We were directed to press for the administration's concurrence with the positions, and to have it all worked out by the afternoon.

Finding a meeting place posed a problem. Maximum secrecy was necessary until an agreement was reached. Members' offices would be unsuitable, as the press was camped there virtually all the time.

We finally decided on booking a room in the Hotel Congressional, and secured room 410 for the following day, October 28, at 9:30 a.m. McCulloch notified Katzenbach of the place, circumstances, and guidelines for the meeting to address the remaining unresolved issues. Katzenbach said that arrangements were fine with him and that the White House was agreeable to most of the Republican demands they had hammered out on Saturday.

As Rep. Lindsay left the office, he informed us that he and Rep. Bromwell had a breakfast session scheduled the following morning with Rep. Corman and Rep. Kastenmeier, to see how the Democrats felt about working out a compromise. And McCulloch, just before going home, placed another call to Minority Leader Halleck.

CHAPTER 12

Last-Minute Problems

October 28, 1963

The morning of Monday, October 28, broke with a number of disturbing items reported in the press and over radio and television. Joseph Alsop's syndicated *New York Herald Tribune* Matter of Fact column of October 28, "The Anti-Legislative Process," deeply disturbed Rep. Lindsay, as much of it was exaggerated and inaccurate.

In his column, Alsop attacked Celler, the Leadership Conference, Black leaders, and liberal posturing for "a bill marked by features of extremely doubtful Constitutionality" and "dead certain to die in the House Rules Committee or to be killed on the House floor." As for "committee members of the Kastenmaier[sic]-Lindsay stripe," he condemned them for not joining the committee's "center group" to re-write a more acceptable bill.

Lindsay's hurried reply—"Setting Alsop Straight," in the *Herald Tribune*'s Letters to the Editor section published the following day—was dashed off at the very moment that our negotiations were underway across the street at the Hotel Congressional.

To the Herald Tribune:

Mr. Alsop's column, "The Anti-Legislative Process," requires comment. Although Mr. Alsop usually speaks authoritatively on these subjects, he has not taken the trouble to check with members of the House Judiciary Committee. Rep. Robert W. Kastenmeier, D., Wis., and I are singled out as uncompromising liberals who are more interested in holding to certain principles than in obtaining constructive legislation.

If Mr. Alsop had taken the trouble to check, possibly we could have enlightened him about the history of current civil rights legislative proposals. He should know that the subcommittee bill for the most part is sound legislation. He should know that all of us who support it in principle understand the need for three or four tightening amendments. Title III, for example, can be brought back into proper shape with a single amendment, which would make it identical to the Title III provision that I and 31 other Republicans introduced last January and which the Attorney General went out of his way to say he had never bothered to read. Title II on public accommodations can be narrowed slightly to be more acceptable to a wider group. These amendments are prepared and can be offered as committee amendments on the floor of the House.

In its present posture, a line-by-line rewriting of the bill in the full Judiciary Committee will take weeks, and in seeking to achieve these amendments we will probably lose all of the public accommodations, most of the voting provisions and all of the provisions on job opportunities.

Meanwhile, the attacks on the subcommittee bill, aided and abetted by members of the press, have not assisted the quiet diplomacy which some of us have been trying to carry on, which might lead in the next few days to a compromise that is not too far removed from the subcommittee bill. Some of these disparaging comments, most especially those that question the bill's Constitutionality, may come back to haunt those who make them when a near-like bill is before the House for debate. They will then be for a strong bill, but they will not have assisted its passage.

Anthony Lewis, on WQXR radio, had been cutting in his comments that morning about Republican efforts on civil rights. Democratic Representative Frank Thompson of New Jersey had appeared on the *Today* show, talking in a similar vein. Their theme was that no one knew what Republicans wanted and that Republicans were traditionally lukewarm on civil rights.

It was about 8:30 a.m. on October 28 when I read Lewis's "Congress Faces Crucial Decision on Civil Rights" in the *New York Times*.

The chances for passage of a civil rights bill in the present session of Congress may be decided this week.

Within the next few days the outcome of the Administration's struggle to get an acceptable bipartisan bill out of the House Judiciary Committee will be known. The decision will affect the entire legislative outlook for the President.

The key figure in the civil rights picture remains the House minority leader, Representative Charles A. Halleck of Indiana.

The Administration believes it must have his agreement to get a bill past the Rules Committee and the House itself. But as of tonight no one seemed to know what, if any, bill he would agree to support.

Panel Bill Opposed

The Judiciary Committee now has before it a subcommittee draft opposed by the Administration as excessive in two respects.

One of these provisions would extend the proposed ban on segregation in public accommodations to places operated under state "authorization, permission or license." The other would allow the Attorney General to sue for alleged violation of any constitutional right.

The Administration's view on the first point was supported today by the committee on Federal legislation of the Association of the Bar of the City of New York.

In a letter, the committee chairman, Fred N. Fishman, said the broadening of the public accommodations section ran "undesirable constitutional risks."

Redrafting Is Problem

Civil rights leaders who have been pressing for a broader bill say privately that they do not think they would have any difficulty agreeing with the Justice Department on the redrafting needed to end Administration objections. Justice Department officials say the same thing.

The difficulty is that the redrafting cannot be done in the 35-member Judiciary Committee. Its meetings have been chaotic sessions of contradictory motions and simultaneous shouting.

The Administration believes, however, that its only hope is to work privately for a firm bipartisan agreement on what the bill should contain and then go to the committee for a vote.

The committee now has before it a motion to report the subcommittee draft out intact. Unless the Administration's strategy produces agreement soon, probably by Tuesday, Northern Democrats and some younger Republicans will produce a majority for this motion as the only way to end the talk.

Kennedy Takes Hand

President Kennedy, who took a personal hand in the fight last week by calling legislators to two White House meetings, may have another session with committee Democrats tomorrow. But the real problem is still getting agreement with the Republicans.

Mr. Halleck has been home duck-hunting this weekend. But the ranking G.O.P. member of the Judiciary Committee, William M. McCulloch of Ohio, has been at work on the problem and has talked with Administration representatives.

The sentence "Mr. Halleck has been home duck-hunting this weekend," immediately caught my eye. It made me angry. First, it was untrue. Rep. Halleck had gone back to his district for a speaking engagement. Actually, he had been in his office throughout much of the weekend, from where he had spoken several times by telephone with Rep. McCulloch. Halleck had been completely informed of the negotiations that McCulloch was carrying on with Deputy Attorney General Katzenbach.

Even if the duck-hunting statement had been accurate, it bore no relevance to a factual account of the bill's status. It was an unfortunate and harmful thing to write, as Halleck and McCulloch had been struggling for weeks to get the administration off the hook—against the determined wishes of a large number of House Republicans. Lewis, a supporter of the administration, was in fact harming it by downgrading Halleck, a person whose cooperation the administration most urgently needed.

It was also unfair to single out Halleck, as there had been other principals in this legislative drama who had truly indulged in recreation that weekend. Manny Celler spent his Saturday nights at the opera. Nick Katzenbach was out on his boat. John Lindsay went to a wedding. What difference did it make? All of them had also spent much of their weekend trying to salvage a civil rights bill. So had Charlie Halleck.

Unfortunately, the whole article read not as an impartial news story, but as an inside report on how the administration viewed its problems in getting its civil rights bill through "its" Judiciary Committee. Reading

Lewis's article—which was combed with phrases such as "the Administration's struggle," "the Administration believes," "opposed by the Administration," "Administration objections," "the Administration's view," and "the Administration's strategy"—one could have concluded that the Kennedy administration was the only party concerned with enacting a civil rights bill.

The *New York Times* journalist made it sound as though no one else was engaged in the struggle to enact civil rights legislation. No one else had views, beliefs, or objections worth bothering about. No one else opposed the subcommittee draft. No one else had a legislative strategy. The Leadership Conference on Civil Rights, as well as Democrats and Republicans in Congress, were of little significance. If they had views, objections, strategies, and beliefs, anyone reading the *Times* that Monday would have hardly been aware of them. Presumably, the views and strategies of these other groups were determined solely by the administration.

Persons noted in the story were those who agreed with the administration. The Committee on Federal Legislation of the Association of the Bar of the City of New York was also cited by Lewis as supporting the administration's position. Publicly, the civil rights leaders were pressing for broader, hence unconstitutional, legislation. But they too sought spiritual union with the administration; according to Lewis, "they say privately that they do not think they would have any difficulty agreeing with the Justice Department on the redrafting needed to end Administration objections. Justice Department officials say the same thing."

If agreement with the administration was the ideal, talking to the administration was considered being "at work on the problem." By that logic, since Rep. McCulloch had spoken with the administration, he had been at work on the problem. Meanwhile, the members of the Judiciary Committee were in a purgatory of "chaotic sessions of contradictory motions and simultaneous shouting."

I also pondered the statement "no one seemed to know what, if any, bill [Halleck] would agree to support." It was common knowledge that Halleck told President Kennedy, back on October 23, of his support for a comprehensive civil rights bill. On the following day, Halleck had told the press that he favored reasonable civil rights legislation. The White House, the Justice Department, Speaker McCormack, Chairman Celler, the Republican leadership, and the GOP members of the Judiciary Committee had known for weeks that Halleck had been working as hard as anyone in the Republican ranks, with the exception of the even harder-working McCulloch, to reach agreement on a measure quite close to the administration's bill.

Lewis was certainly aware of this. Perhaps from his perspective, "what, if any, bill" could only mean 100 percent support for the administration bill—the only bill that mattered. Since Halleck was not a 100 percent administration supporter, it implied that he had no position on civil rights. Apparently, support of the administration was the only position one could have and still be in favor of enacting civil rights legislation.

Lewis also imbued Halleck with powers that he never possessed, positioning him as "the key figure in the civil rights picture" whose agreement was necessary "to get a bill past the Rules Committee." This statement was based on the erroneous idea that the top and the top alone makes policy.

Charles Halleck was the Republican floor leader and spokesman for the House Republicans. It was only on the House floor that the full weight of his leadership would be felt. As floor leader, he was responsible for determining floor strategy. But he did not determine legislative policy for the party. That policy was generally formed instead by the majority of the Republican members of the committee having jurisdiction over the legislation in question.

Initially, Republican decisions on civil rights were made by Republicans on the Judiciary Committee. The most influential were McCulloch and Lindsay. The Republican members of the Judiciary Committee took the initiative in introducing legislation that bore the party's stamp. They framed the party's major pronouncements on civil rights. They drafted its replies to administrative positions and Democratic attacks. They had done so from the beginning of the 88th Congress. Although they consulted Halleck and sought his counsel at every turn, he never tried to dissuade them from a course of action once a majority of the committee Republicans were set on making a move.

Yet it would seem that the Republican method of reaching agreement did not conform to Lewis's preconceived model, so he rejected it out of hand and refused to give any credence to what he was told by Republicans.

Furthermore, Halleck did not dominate the Rules Committee or Republican sentiment in the House itself.

Decisions of the Republican members of the House Rules Committee were made by the Republican members of the House Rules Committee. Rep. Brown of Ohio, the ranking Republican, was the leader there.

Finally, for Lewis, the initial problem was not getting the bill past the Rules Committee and the House floor, but getting it through the House Judiciary Committee. According to Lewis, the administration had a solution for this: It wanted to write a bill itself—one that would bypass the committee, permitting only the formality of a vote.

It is clear, then, why Lewis centered his attention almost exclusively on the administration, virtually ignoring and in fact downgrading the significance of the other participants in the legislative struggle—notably, the members of the House Judiciary Committee. For Lewis, the Judiciary was of less significance because, he believed, the civil rights bill would not be written there. He viewed the committee as merely an adjunct of the administration.

As I headed for McCulloch's office that morning, I wondered how the article would have seemed if wherever Lewis had printed the words "the Administration," instead the words "the House Republicans" had appeared in their place. It would have given an equally distorted view of events.

McCulloch was visibly angry about the *Times* story. Nevertheless, he said, the meeting with Katzenbach and Marshall should be held as planned. Our discussion of the *Times* and the other disturbing media stories subsided, however, when McCulloch's assistant, Vera Page, informed him that Rep. Halleck was on the phone from his home in Rensselaer, Indiana.

Halleck was so angry and so loud that I could hear some of what he was saying. Either he had seen the early edition of the *Times* or someone had called it to his attention. He began the conversation by calling Lewis a "no-good" something-or-other. McCulloch tried to calm him down, but Halleck continued his outburst. He warned McCulloch, surely thinking of our upcoming meeting at the Hotel Congressional, not to bind him to any agreement on the bill.

"If this is the kind of rot the administration is feeding Lewis, then I'm not going to be a party to any agreement," Halleck continued. "The boys on our side are mad as hell at me for being willing to work something out. It's bad enough I'm accused of doing the dirty work for the White House. I sure don't have to get kicked in the teeth in the bargain."

Halleck said he would return from Indiana that afternoon, and it would be necessary to call a meeting of the committee Republicans for the following morning, October 29, to determine what course of action should be adopted.

As Copenhaver and I prepared to leave for our meeting at the Congressional, Katzenbach's office called to advise McCulloch that Katzenbach and Marshall would arrive at the hotel a little late, at about 10:00 a.m. McCulloch decided to accompany us there. He said he thought he ought to say a few words to them about the unfortunate stories in the press.

As we were walking over, McCulloch asked me a surprising question. "Bob, do you know if Anthony Lewis and the attorney general are close friends?"

I said I was quite sure they were. "You know, I live in McLean," I told McCulloch. "So do Lewis and the attorney general. There is a young woman who lives maybe one hundred yards from me who has done some babysitting for the Lewis family. She said there were a number of calls back and forth between Lewis and the attorney general, often in the evening—"

McCulloch stopped me there. "You know how hard Lewis is being on Halleck," he said. "Now I think I may know why. You recall the incidents at the time Libby [Libonati] withdrew his amendment. You heard me warn the attorney general about that."

"Yes," I replied.

"You also know the AG later said I had never warned him. And then, after our conversation, he changed that story to say he *had* told Burke Marshall about it. But you recall that Marshall told me he never knew about it—the attorney general had never told him."

I said, yes, of course I recalled all of that.

"You may recall also how I told Charlie Halleck about it," McCulloch continued, "and how we agreed that under the circumstances, it would be impossible to negotiate further with the attorney general. Charlie spoke with the president, who said, 'Okay, my brother doesn't have to be involved.' Well, last week at the White House, Nick Katzenbach was present. Lyndon Johnson was present too. But not the attorney general."

McCulloch was now certain that the attorney general was very angry at Rep. Halleck over the Libonati amendment debacle, and that he had conveyed his anger and vindictiveness to Lewis—who had carefully injected this antagonism into his newspaper report.

*   *   *

The stakes were high. Two previous agreements on proposed civil rights legislation had already fallen through. If the Democrats failed to honor this one, the GOP rank-and-file would prevent their leaders from making another attempt at a compromise—and this 88th Congress would be unable to pass any civil rights legislation at all.

The question now was, what would happen at the Hotel Congressional? And would it make enough of a difference?

CHAPTER 13

"It Could Go Either Way"
October 28, 1963

The Hotel Congressional, conveniently located just across the street from the House office buildings, served as a gathering place and sometimes even living quarters for US representatives. We had decided to hold the meeting there, away from offices on the Hill, because it was crucial to avoid disclosure until an accord had been reached.

Ironically, the room we had rented was directly across the hall from the Republican Congressional Campaign Committee office. This was unintended, and upon arriving at about 9:45 a.m. and discovering the room's location, Rep. McCulloch, Copenhaver, and I thought it might upset Deputy AG Katzenbach and Assistant AG Marshall.

McCulloch had decided that perhaps the problem with AG Kennedy and Anthony Lewis would not be all that important in the end, but he still planned to say something about it to the two Justice Department officials, whom he respected. At 10:00 a.m., Katzenbach and Marshall arrived and shook our hands. McCulloch immediately began by saying that Rep. Halleck had been upset by the Lewis story in the *Times*, and that almost all Republicans were disturbed by what appeared to be stories planted in the press to downgrade Republican efforts in seeking civil rights legislation.

"I have worked closely these many months with John Lindsay, who has been so helpful and constructive at all times, and without whose thorough, intelligent, and able work yesterday we would not be as far along as we are," McCulloch continued. "He was deeply offended by the Alsop column, the Lewis article, and other such stories. They have not been helpful."

It was the feeling of many Republicans, I added, that if Lewis did not do a fairer job of reporting news on the civil rights bill, they would request of the *New York Times* to assign another reporter to cover the story.

Katzenbach denied having spoken to Alsop and said he was sorry to hear about Lewis's comments regarding Halleck.

McCulloch went back across the street to his office. Dave Filvaroff, Katzenbach's assistant, arrived soon thereafter and briefly joined the discussions.

The purpose of the meeting was to seek agreement on the outstanding issues dividing the McCulloch–Lindsay position from the Department of Justice stance, of which there were perhaps seven: (1) Would Title I create a temporary referee provision (as sought by the administration) or a three-judge court proposal (put forward by the Republicans)? (2) Would there be a Part III—and if so, what kind? (3) Would there be a Community Relations Service? (4) Would the life of the Civil Rights Commission be extended for four years or made permanent? (5) Would the power of the Civil Rights Commission be broadened to include instances of vote fraud? (6) What kind of authority would be given to a Federal Employment Practices Commission? (7) Would the census provision on registration and voting statistics remain in the bill?

These were the few remaining issues out of the multitude of questions that had divided the administration and the Judiciary Republicans less than a month before. Obviously, much ground had already been covered.

In room 410, Katzenbach began to question Copenhaver and me on the various points, starting with Title V: We still insisted on a permanent Civil Rights Commission. We restated our opposition to the Community Relations Service. Copenhaver stressed Republican concern that the Civil Rights Commission must have added authority to investigate instances of vote fraud.

Furthermore, he said, a great deal of language in the employment section (Title VII) had to be cleaned up. Katzenbach asked Filvaroff to work with us on that point.

In Title I, we also stressed our hope that the administration would abandon its opposition to the three-judge court provision. Marshall replied that the three-judge proposal would not be received well in Mississippi and probably in Alabama either. Inclusion of this provision, he said, would take the already damaged relations among the judges of the Fifth Circuit and strain them to the breaking point.

Lindsay and the civil rights groups had remained insistent about some kind of Title III in the bill—if not power to initiate civil suits, at least intervention authority for the Department of Justice. When I expressed this to Marshall, he said that the administration was opposed to any separate Title III, as all necessary authority was contained (in their opinion) in the bill's other sections. I replied with the truth: that unless some kind of Title III was included in this compromise bill, it might be impossible to achieve support from the Leadership Conference on Civil Rights and from many House Democrats.

According to Katzenbach, the president still thought Title VIII—the census provision—would be too expensive, even in its revised compromise form, which limited the authority of the Department of Commerce to gather voting and registration statistics to those areas specified by the Civil Rights Commission. But, he added, the administration would not object if the Republicans insisted on its inclusion.

After about 30 minutes of discussion, the room telephone rang. We were all startled. Who could have possibly known we were there?

"You'd better answer it," Katzenbach told me.

"Hello, Bob," said McCulloch's familiar voice when I picked up the phone. "Now, is there anything I can have sent up to you? Maybe Nick and Burke would like some refreshment."

"Okay, sir, I'll ask them."

"How are you doing?"

"We're coming close."

"I want you to come to my office as soon as you are through."

McCulloch's call had broken the tension. We ordered coffee from downstairs and finished the unresolved questions not long afterwards. Katzenbach said they would let McCulloch know in the afternoon whether the president would agree to our demands on the disputed issues.

We chatted amiably on how the bill had gotten so snafued. Katzenbach said they had tried very hard, with White House Congressional Relations Chief Larry O'Brien's help, to persuade Chairman Celler and the Leadership Conference to adopt a more bipartisan approach. "I can understand the civil rights groups' position," Katzenbach conceded. "They're fighting hard for what they believe in. But Celler has been impossible to deal with. One moment, he promises us he agrees with our position. The next moment, he gives the same promise to the Leadership Conference."

Marshall, who had been making some notes, read us a proposed draft of a new Part III that would enable Attorney General Kennedy to intervene in, but not initiate, civil suits in instances where a person was deprived of civil rights.

"What do you think?" he asked.

"That's the bare minimum," we replied.

"Okay," Marshall said, "we'll have it at the 4:00 p.m. meeting with the committee Democrats. Let's see if we need to use it."

Katzenbach said the Justice Department would have everything typed up and mimeographed later in the day, and at that, the meeting broke up. We all returned to our offices.

It was 11:30 a.m., and we had a long day ahead of us.

*   *   *

During Rep. Lindsay's Monday breakfast session, he had found Democratic Representatives Corman and Kastenmeier willing to discuss some kind of compromise bill, as long as it retained the principal parts of the subcommittee bill. Lindsay also spent part of the morning on his reply to the Alsop article, but devoted a larger part to denying rumors that a major "sellout" was imminent on the civil rights bill. And he spoke with Republican Representatives Cahill and MacGregor, who were receptive to going along with some kind of substitute but strongly felt that it should not be called "the administration bill."

For my part, I spoke with Bill Higgs of SNCC, David Cohen of ADA, Clarence Mitchell of NAACP, George Agree of the National Committee for an Effective Congress, Bill Phillips of the Democratic Study Group, Meg Greenfield of *The Reporter*, and Ann Blair of Triangle Publications. To each, I said the same thing: There was nothing new yet.

I had promised to keep the most recent discussions entirely secret. Still, it was hard to avoid press attention.

An Associated Press dispatch released around noon reported on "efforts to reach bipartisan agreement" before a vote the next day on "a bill the administration fears would alienate the moderate Republicans needed to help pass it." When Copenhaver and I met for lunch, he revealed that he had been bombarded by calls and was now certain that the Department of Justice was telling Lewis everything.

"What are they going to do?" I replied. "They need the *Times*'s support much more than they need us. Maybe not for the next few days, but surely for the life of this administration."

By early afternoon, the air was filled with rumors. The Justice Department had told the press that Katzenbach and Marshall were on the Hill. Unable to find them, the press suspected that secret meetings were in progress. By 3:00 p.m., however, there was still no official word on anything.

* * *

At about that time, reporters Beckler, Sawislak, and Sullivan called. They heard that something was up—that an agreement was near. Celler, Rogers, Libonati, and Lindsay all had confirmed it for them, to one degree or another. I asked them, off the record, to please hold off for a few more hours.

"Yes, we're close," I admitted, "but differences still exist. It's a long way from being wrapped up." I added that I might be able to say more at around 6:00 p.m., but I was pledged to secrecy until an understanding had been reached.

Higgs and Cohen came by the office at about 3:30 p.m., worried about a sellout. They said the Judiciary's northern Democrats would soon be leaving for the White House with the understanding that they were going to be pressed into going along with a White House–Republican agreement.

"No agreement yet," I repeated, pointing out that it was impossible to predict what either the White House or the Judiciary Republicans would do.

At about 3:45 p.m., McCulloch phoned to ask me to bring over all the Anthony Lewis clips I had. He said, "I want to look them over in light of our conversation this morning."

At some point while I was in McCulloch's office, from 4:15 p.m. to 4:45 p.m., Copenhaver called. The Department of Justice had accepted everything, including vote fraud and the three-judge court.

I went back to my office. McCulloch called—I noted the time, at 5:26 p.m.—to say that Katzenbach had relayed word to him from the White House. A substantial majority of the northern Democrats indicated they would go along with the substitute bill.

McCulloch then asked me to come to his office and remain there until the end of the day. Because of his experience with Attorney General Kennedy, he said he wanted me to hear every word he uttered and be able to verify every call he made and received.

I made it to his office by 5:30 p.m.

The first call was from Lindsay, who was at Washington National Airport on his way to New York City for an evening of speeches. He planned to return to Washington late that night. McCulloch told him there would be a meeting at the whip's office at 8:30 a.m. the next day, to reach a decision on the substitute. McCulloch urged Lindsay to be there, saying that without Lindsay's strong support, it would be very difficult to obtain the agreement of a majority of the committee's Republicans.

McCulloch then placed a call to Chairman Byrnes of the House Republican Policy Committee. McCulloch brought Byrnes up to date on the day's occurrences and asked whether he knew of the meeting planned for the following morning.

Celler called next. He expressed cautious optimism on the response of his northern colleagues to the White House–offered compromise. He told McCulloch that it looked as if they were going to make it. McCulloch told Celler that he felt a majority of the Judiciary Republicans would now oppose the Moore motion to report out the subcommittee bill.

Throughout the late afternoon, McCulloch repeatedly tried to reach Rep. Brown of the Rules Committee, who had indicated support for the Moore motion. He was unsuccessful, as Brown had gone to the hospital to be with his wife, who was in critical condition.

Rep. Moore phoned in to tell McCulloch that he would not withdraw his motion. If it were defeated, the West Virginia Republican said he would vote against the substitute bill. McCulloch spoke with him at great length, but Moore refused to alter his position. Even an invitation to the White House would not sway him from his course, he claimed.

According to Moore, the vote would be very close.

McCulloch then reached Halleck at his Capitol office. He informed Halleck of Moore's position and of what had occurred during the late afternoon. Halleck said that he would make no commitments until after the meeting with Judiciary and leadership Republicans the next morning.

By this time—6:30 p.m.—the Rat Pack had shown up. Bob Abernathy of NBC, Arnie Sawislak of UPI, John Beckler of AP, Peter Kumpa of the *Baltimore Sun*, and Richard Lyons of the *Washington Post* were stretched out on the chairs and sofas in McCulloch's office, kidding with him, hoping he would tell them what was going on.

McCulloch evaded their queries as best he could.

The reporters shook their heads and laughed. Beckler spoke up: "Bill, are you going to give us another mushy statement?"

McCulloch smiled and said, "Now, John, I can say to all of you that we have made considerable progress in the last 20 minutes. Boys, I don't know about you, but I have worked hard these last few days, and so have many others."

After more laughter and some light banter, they departed.

The day's final call to McCulloch came from Katzenbach, saying that all seemed well. Copies of the substitute bill would be distributed to the homes of all committee members—southerners included—by 9:00 or 10:00 that evening.

Three crucial meetings were scheduled for Tuesday morning: First, at 8:30 a.m., the House Judiciary Republicans and the Republican leadership would gather in the

Capitol office of Rep. Arends, the party whip. Then, if a majority of those present agreed to support the compromise and vote against the pending Moore motion, Halleck and McCulloch would go to the White House to inform the president. Finally, Halleck and McCulloch would return immediately to the Hill, where the House Judiciary Committee meeting would convene at 10:30 a.m.

It was long after midnight when I received a phone call from a Democratic friend. "It's not in the bag," he warned me. "A lot of our guys are not going to go along."

"How close do you think it will be?" I asked.

His reply: "It could go either way."

CHAPTER 14

The Vote
October 29, 1963

Promptly at 8:30 a.m. the next day, Tuesday, October 29, the meeting of the Judiciary Republicans and the Republican Party leadership got underway in the whip's office at the Capitol. I saw Rep. Cahill and Rep. MacGregor just as they were about to enter the room. Both were of the same opinion as my late-night caller: The outcome could go either way.

I headed to my office and then returned to the Capitol, arriving there a little after 9:30 a.m. The meeting broke up a few minutes later, and I quickly learned of the events in the whip's office.

Rep. McCulloch spoke in favor of the substitute

agreement—including the provisions hammered out in room 410 with Katzenbach and Marshall. Rep. Moore spoke against it, urging continued support for his motion to report the October 22 subcommittee bill.

Rep. Lindsay delivered a strong speech in support of McCulloch, which was no surprise to me after he had called me from his home at 1:30 a.m., having just returned from New York. Although it was the middle of the night, I made sure to recount everything I knew.

"No matter what happens tomorrow, I'm going to stick with McCulloch," Lindsay had vowed to me over the phone. "That guy has given his all on this. I have to support him."

In the whip's office, Lindsay asserted that the substitute was a better bill than the subcommittee measure. Liberal Republicans Cahill, Mathias, and MacGregor indicated they would support McCulloch's compromise bill, although not without misgivings. On the other side, southern Republicans Cramer and Poff supported Moore.

Everyone in the room expressed deep concern that the administration would get all the credit for the agreement and would trade away the hard-won Republican language as soon as it could. Rep. Meader of Michigan wasn't having any of it; he said he would oppose the Moore motion *and* the substitute. He felt that both measures contained provisions he could not support.

Minority Leader Halleck called for an informal vote of the committee Republicans: 8–6 in support of the substitute.

"That's it!" Halleck said to me. "That's enough for me to go to the White House." He planned to tell the president that a majority of Republicans on the House Judiciary Committee would support the substitute in committee that day. "I guess we finally made it a bipartisan bill. I sure hope we're doing the right thing."

While the meeting was in progress, however, I had received a call from the SNCC's Higgs, who had the confidence of Rep. Corman and Rep. Kastenmeier on the Democratic side. Higgs asked, "What will Lindsay and Cahill do if not enough Democrats support the package?"

"They'll still vote for it," I replied.

"I don't know if there are enough votes for the package to win. Kastenmeier, Rogers, and Libonati all plan to vote for the Moore motion," he said, before adding Representative Jacob Gilbert of New York and Representative Don Edwards of California to this tally of Democrats. "Corman will vote for the substitute if Lindsay does; otherwise he'll oppose it."

"If the southerners all vote for the Moore motion," I said, "we may have only a single vote to spare. If one person switches his position, the Moore motion might still carry."

"That's exactly what I'm saying," Higgs replied, and I promised to convey the information to Lindsay, Halleck, and McCulloch.

I sought out McCulloch and Lindsay as they left the whip's office. To McCulloch, I gave a list of the northern Democrats who planned to stick with the Moore motion. He showed it to Halleck, who said that by his count, the Moore motion could be defeated by as much as two votes—but even that would make things too close for comfort.

Apparently, we learned, even Cahill's support was not that firm. Copenhaver was going over the substitute legislation with him at that very moment.

Halleck told McCulloch that he would have to put it to the president to round up the necessary votes. Otherwise, there would be some seriously embarrassed leaders in the House that day.

As they prepared to leave the Capitol, Halleck turned to Lindsay and Mathias. "You fellows better buoy up the other members. This thing is going to be damn close."

With those words, Halleck and McCulloch left the Capitol, got into Halleck's limousine, and headed for the White House. They were there for only a few minutes, seeing the president briefly.

Halleck said that a majority of the committee Republicans—eight of 14—favored the substitute bill, and in a separate vote a larger majority would oppose the Moore motion. President Kennedy assured Halleck there would be enough votes for the substitute to pass.

Halleck also said that his support for the substitute today did not imply a commitment to a Federal Employment Practices Commission when the bill reached the floor. He simply said that he hadn't made up his mind on that one. The president thanked them for all they had done, and they exchanged pleasantries before Halleck and McCulloch departed.

At 10:00 a.m., I met with NAACP's Mitchell, who was very angry. He said we were making a big mistake by supporting the substitute. The subcommittee bill was better, he insisted, and he was sure it could pass the House if the Republican leadership stayed with it.

"It isn't only Republicans you could lose," I replied. "It's border-state and conservative Democrats—enough to delay a rule on the bill and weaken its chances of clearing the House without being gutted. I know the bill should be stronger," I added, "but it is a lot stronger than any of us ever believed possible. It really is our best chance."

* * *

The meeting of the House Judiciary Committee began soon after 10:30 a.m. There was pandemonium in the halls as cameramen, reporters, lobbyists, and interested people, from all over the Hill and beyond, thronged the passageways outside the ornate committee room.

I stationed myself with the reporters who, hungry for information, pressed into the office adjoining the committee room, where they were cordially received by committee staff members Anne Berger and Jane Caldwell. In the adjacent room—Chairman Celler's outer office—his secretaries, Minnie White and Alba Kidd, abandoned all hope of answering any mail that morning and offered coffee to Nick Katzenbach, Burke Marshall, and their deputies Bill Geoghegan, Joe Dolan, and Dave Filvaroff.

Katzenbach and Marshall then moved into Celler's private office and opened up phone lines to the Justice Department and the White House. Celler's office, which I had seen a few times, was filled with mementos from more than four decades of congressional service. Pictures of presidents, from Harding through Kennedy, adorned the walls, along with those of friends and colleagues of bygone days and the present. A photograph of Celler gazing wistfully into the eyes of Italian film actress Sophia Loren had pride of place.

Before the Judiciary meeting began, I learned that earlier in the morning, a group of Democrats had met in Celler's office to review the strategy mapped out by Celler; his counsel, Bill Foley; Congressmen Rodino and Brooks; and the Justice Department. Who would make which motion, and when? How much time would be consumed? They went over these questions and more, working from an actual script, rehearsing until they were certain of each step they would take when the meeting began. The principal onus would be on Celler, who rose to the occasion.

Within minutes after the committee meeting had begun, Bess Dick, Celler's faithful assistant and chief of staff for many years, came out of the committee room and whispered a few words to Deputy AG Katzenbach. Katzenbach flashed a big smile and informed us that Moore's motion had been defeated by a vote of 19–15. (One committee member was absent that day.)

In the halls, though no announcement had yet been made of any committee action, excitement was building. By then, committee counsel Bill Foley had already begun to read the substitute that Chairman Celler had offered in place of the defeated subcommittee bill supported by Rep. Moore. Now the question was, would the substitute bill pass the full Judiciary Committee?

News soon began to spread. Inside the committee room, objections were being raised: Celler was going to call for a quick vote on the substitute, without allowing any opportunity for an explanation, a discussion, or amendments.

Frankly, I was surprised that Celler would act so quickly.

At 11:45 a.m., Foley completed his reading of the bill. According to those present, points of order were immediately raised. There were demands for recognition . . . motions to recommit . . . requests for the regular order . . . shouts and commotion . . . members pounding ashtrays on the tables, demanding to be heard.

But all the ruckus was ignored. With the clock ticking toward noon, when the House would convene, Celler spoke for less than a minute in support of the substitute. Then he yielded to McCulloch, who consumed barely 15 seconds. McCulloch, in turn, yielded to Rodino, who moved to cut off debate over the outcries of the southerners.

Celler asked Bess Dick to call the roll for a vote.

When the noon bell rang, members charged out of the committee room. Many were shaking their heads in disbelief.

The press poured in. Although no vote had yet been announced, everyone present soon learned that the substitute had carried, 20–14.

It felt like a win, even though Celler would need to reconvene the committee later in the afternoon, as soon as the House adjourned, in order to take a second vote to report the bill formally. Celler and McCulloch, Democrat and Republican, were smiling as they posed for pictures and submitted to numerous interviews.

The hall outside the committee room was bathed in light and filled with hubbub. McCulloch praised the chairman, the president, Katzenbach and Marshall, John Lindsay, Charlie Halleck, his loyal and dedicated staff, and the press. Assistant AG Marshall announced that there would be a press briefing on the bill at 1:00 p.m. at the Department of Justice.

I felt enormously relieved. After all that work—all those hours, phone calls, and back-and-forth negotiations—America was close to having a civil rights bill that we truly hoped would soon become law.

Copenhaver and I grabbed a quick sandwich, then went by taxi to the Justice Department and headed to the fifth floor. When we learned that the press briefing had been postponed to 2:00 p.m., we went for coffee. Upon our return, Marshall asked us to come to his office. He said the attorney general wanted to meet us before the press briefing.

We shook hands with Kennedy, who was cordial to us. I noticed that his office had a number of his children's drawings on the walls. I also noticed that he wore white tennis socks—something I often did too, unfashionable as it was in 1963.

When the press briefing began, the attorney general introduced Copenhaver and me, since we were not customarily present at these meetings. He asked Copenhaver to comment as to whether anything was unclear or omitted in the meeting of the Judiciary Committee.

Then, with courtesy and restraint, Kennedy, Katzenbach, and Marshall explained the new bill. About 60 reporters were present. All questions, no matter how obvious or trivial, were dealt with in patient good humor.

About two-thirds of the way through the briefing, Copenhaver and I received a phone call from Bess Dick.

The House had adjourned. Chairman Celler wanted to reconvene the Judiciary Committee within 30 minutes to conclude action on the bill.

A group of us, armed with copies of the bill, rode back to the Hill in Katzenbach's car. When we got to the committee room, Bess asked me very nicely if I would help her distribute the copies for the members.

A few minutes before 3:00 p.m., the door to Chairman Celler's private office opened. Celler, Peter Rodino, and Jack Brooks emerged arm in arm, laughing. Celler sang to the tune of "Camptown Races"—but with words that sounded like "Peter's gonna ring the bell, doodah, doodah."

I learned afterwards that inside the committee room, Celler had apologized to his colleagues for the way he had acted during the morning session. He blamed his behavior on the unbelievable amount of pressure to which he had been subjected from many quarters. When he finished his explanation, Rep. Forrester joked, "Oh, let's take the committee picture now, Mr. Chairman, so my constituents can see where I was when lightning struck."

The bill was ordered reported, by a vote of 23–11.

*   *   *

Outside the Judiciary Committee room, a number of interested participants lingered. Clarence Mitchell was visibly upset. Joseph Rauh and the ILGWU's Evelyn Dubrow seemed less annoyed than Mitchell. The ADA's David Cohen said he was mildly disappointed. They had hoped that the subcommittee bill, which was arguably a stronger piece of civil rights legislation, could hold enough supporters to have passed. But Bill Higgs of SNCC was happy with the results. He said he thought his colleagues would be happier when they realized that this bill was much better than the original Kennedy bill—and far stronger than anything McCulloch and Halleck would have been expected to support.

Copenhaver and I stayed for quite a while, talking to Higgs, Cohen, the AP's John Beckler, Andy Glass of the *Herald Tribune*, Murray Kempton of the *New Republic*, and Jack Beidler of the AFL-CIO. I broke away to use the committee phone and spoke to Eugenia Daugherty in Representative Cahill's office, Steve Kurzman in Senator Javits's office, and Ethel Maness and Barbara Nash, in the respective offices of Representative Leonard Farbstein and Representative Ogden Reid, both of New York. Whenever I could, I pointed out that Lindsay and McCulloch, the two most unhappy Republican participants in the subcommittee deliberations, were the members who had been instrumental in pulling together both the contents and support for the substitute bill.

Before I left for home to monitor the television and radio coverage of the day's happenings, I had one more conversation with Mitchell, who sharply criticized what he called "shabby tactics used to get the bill out." I said the same thing would have been true had the subcommittee bill been approved. Neither bill was discussed as open to amendment.

To the broader public, television reports were hailing the committee action as a triumph of the administration. *The Huntley–Brinkley Report* on NBC that night began with the words "The Kennedy administration won its fight . . ." Likewise, Walter Cronkite opened his CBS newscast with "President Kennedy got the House Judiciary Committee to go along . . ." "Republicans helped" was but a subsidiary theme in these broadcasts.

Later responses to the action of the committee were fairly predictable. Most northern journals were favorable to the compromise and very favorable to the administration. Of the hundreds of pieces I read in the weeks to come, only a minority emphasized the bipartisan nature of the triumph.

The manner in which the bill was voted out of the committee, however, was bitterly attacked. Many Republicans joined southern Democrats in objecting to the haste with which the measure was "railroaded" through the committee without opportunity for debate or amendment.

The committee majority was silent on the procedures used to approve the substitute measure, but there was a widespread feeling among all those involved that the committee had acted improperly.

The bill that was ordered reported by the House Judiciary Committee had not been drafted by that committee. It had been drafted in secret meetings—including the one I participated in at the Hotel Congressional, room 410—by the Department of Justice and the Republican congressmen McCulloch and Lindsay, based on what they believed would be a reasonable consensus of the Judiciary Committee.

Yet in truth, members of the Judiciary Committee did not have adequate time to read and consider the substitute legislation. Practically no opportunity was afforded for discussion of the measure. It was approved in almost total disregard of the normal principles of due process and legislative fairness, with one exception: an amendment on Title I (voting) proposed by Rep. Meader—to establish a commission to consider enforcing Section 2 of the 14th Amendment—which was quickly voted down. Had it been approved as an amendment to the substitute bill, the Meader amendment would have had more sweeping implications than almost anything in the subcommittee bill itself.

The full committee did not even discuss such important subjects as accommodations, employment, education, and the withholding of federal funds.

I didn't realize until later that night that something was wrong with the way the bill had been considered and the way I had gone along with a hasty procedure that I really deplored. But by then it was midnight, and after all, it had been a very long day.

CHAPTER 15

Aftermath

October 30–November 21, 1963

On Wednesday, October 30, Republican Representative Steven Derounian of New York brought an umbrella onto the House floor and placed it on the minority leader's desk. Since British Prime Minister Neville Chamberlain's capitulation to Adolf Hitler at Munich, the umbrella had become a symbol used to criticize leaders who were seen to be appeasing their opponents. Leaving one on Charlie Halleck's desk indicated the anger felt by many of the Republican rank and file at their leaders for getting the administration off the hook on civil rights.

A large number of Republicans had seen political capital to be gained in taking the subcommittee bill to the

House floor, where it would have to be watered down—by the Democrats—if the administration wanted any chance of its being passed. Or they foresaw that passage of the "strong" subcommittee bill would help the GOP by alienating whites, especially in the South, from the Democrats heading into the 1964 elections.

The anger of these hostile Republicans was intensified by the numerous press reports that lavished praise on the administration for getting the civil rights bill out of the House Judiciary Committee. The truth was that the Republicans on the committee had played a pivotal role in breaking the deadlock that had threatened passage of the bill. Many of their colleagues deeply resented seeing the Kennedys receive all the credit for getting the bill out of the committee.

The umbrella on Rep. Halleck's desk was a reminder to the Republican leadership that a number of members felt the party would gain nothing by the statesmanship of Halleck, McCulloch, and the rest.

By day's end, the strident voices of discontent had swelled to a mighty chorus of unconcealed bitterness. At lunch in the Capitol dining room, those who had opposed the Moore motion and supported the substitute bill were greeted with boos, jeers, and cries of "sellout" and "traitor." The brunt of the abuse was borne, of course, by Lindsay, McCulloch, and Halleck. Although there were exceptions, the most vocal among the discontented were members of the party's right wing. Some were members who would have voted against any civil rights bill, no matter the content.

Late in the day, I met Rep. Brown outside the New (Longworth) House Office Building. He described the action of the committee Republicans in voting down the Moore motion as "shit in the nest." Halleck and McCulloch, in his opinion, should have forced the administration to make greater concessions to the Republican position. Rep. Brown argued that this approach would have strengthened his hand with GOP members when the bill came before the Rules Committee, where he was the ranking Republican.

By evening, the Republican dissidents had already acted. Representative Durward "Doc" Hall of Missouri called for a breakfast meeting of interested Republicans the following morning in the Presidential Room of the Hotel Congressional.

Other reactions to the substitute bill varied. The press continued to be strongly favorable to the compromise and the administration. David Cohen told me the ADA was not happy but recognized that things could have been worse. The Republican Party, he indicated, had made great progress in its attitude toward civil rights. But Sid Zagri of the Teamsters really bawled me out. "The Republicans have put the manacles of statesmanship on the administration," he said, describing the compromise as "a great political blunder."

Rep. Lindsay seemed pleased but was worried about "many angry Republicans." Sen. Javits was, according to staffer Steve Kurzman, fairly happy. Diane Le Baker of Republican Senator Leversett Saltonstall's office suggested we put together an analysis showing what the Republicans contributed to the bill. This would provide a way for Republicans—who, as the minority party, got less attention—to highlight their input.

I had a long talk in the afternoon with *Time* magazine's Loye Miller, who asked a tough question: "How hard are the southerners going to fight the bill?" I responded that they would do their best to make the bill look much tougher, affording more rights to Blacks than it did, to justify their opposition.

McCulloch asked me over to his office to discuss the Chamberlain umbrella. He expressed tremendous gratitude to Lindsay for standing with him. "I know it would have been easy for him to take the more political course and support the subcommittee bill," he acknowledged, "particularly since he would have received so much praise from the civil rights groups." He urged me to monitor the next day's breakfast meeting of the angry House Republicans.

About 60 of those Republicans assembled on October 31 for their supposedly secret breakfast session at the Hotel Congressional. I was not there, but some who were present told me that those who came for the eggs and coffee heard a number of speakers lambaste the party leadership for reaching a civil rights accord with the White House and the Democratic majority—without seeking input from non-committee Republicans, who wanted to see Democrats bear responsibility for watering down a strong bill. It was clear that a campaign issue was more important to these Republicans than was the enactment of lasting, meaningful civil rights legislation.

They were disturbed by the way the party leadership, chiefly Halleck and McCulloch, had reached a decision to support a compromise with the Kennedy administration.

Some criticized Halleck for not consulting the Republican Policy Committee or bringing the matter before a conference of all House Republicans.

Among those attending the meeting were Judiciary Republicans Poff, Cramer, Moore, King, and Patrick Minor Martin (Republican of California), who regaled the assemblage on the high-handed way the bill was rammed down the throats of the Judiciary Committee. Also present were Representative Clarence Brown, Representative Katharine St. George of New York, and Representative H. Allen Smith of California, three of the five Republicans on the House Rules Committee. Noticeably absent were Gerald Ford, John Byrnes, Leslie Arends, and Melvin Laird, the party leaders who presumably had not been consulted on the meeting, most likely because it was known they were not opposed to the current legislation.

I learned afterwards that no agreement of any kind was reached at the 90-minute gathering. Rep. Brown was especially influential in encouraging his fellow Republicans not to take any action. While stating his disagreement with what McCulloch and Halleck had done, he said that he and the other leaders had known what was going on from having attended a number of meetings on the question. He objected more to what Halleck did than to the way he had done it.

Some reports described the meeting as a serious threat to Halleck's House minority leadership. Yet nothing materialized in that direction for the remainder of the 88th Congress. Most of the criticism of Halleck was merely anger at a lost opportunity to make the Democratic administration look bad.

Lindsay and McCulloch were quick to realize, however, that this anger might create obstacles for the civil rights bill. Eager to forestall this problem, they sought out Halleck in the afternoon.

Halleck told Lindsay that he and others should speak out as forcefully as they could in support of the substitute legislation. He told them there might have been political advantage for a while in blocking the bill, but in the end, it would have backfired against the party. "All we have to do around here is let the word out that we're studying an administration bill, and the press blasts hell out of us," he explained. "Within a week, all our faces would have been red."

Nevertheless, they all realized that the militant response of these Republicans was no temporary headache. Halleck was well aware that "the boys mean business." As a result, two decisions were made. First, because of his favorable relations with the press, Lindsay was asked to do all he could to persuade them to present the Republicans' civil rights actions fairly. "The other thing we're going to need," said Halleck, "is some kind of document showing all the changes that Republicans got written into the bill. As soon as the boys can send something to their districts showing that this was as much our bill as the administration's, most of them will begin to quiet down."

On the way back to my office, I saw Frank Meyer, Rep. Ford's administrative assistant. Meyer said that Ford knew about Doc Hall's meeting but hadn't gone and was sticking with Halleck.

I knew President Kennedy was planning a news conference and I was worried about a quick resurgence of partisanship. I telephoned Nick Katzenbach in the Deputy AG's office, and we discussed the press reaction to the administration's victory. I told him about the Chamberlain umbrella and the anti-Halleck breakfast. Katzenbach asked what we wanted him to do and whether I was speaking for McCulloch and Halleck.

"Absolutely," I said, and I explained they felt it was important for the president to talk about continuing support for a broad-based bipartisan bill. Anything less would be interpreted as meaning the House Republicans had been conned. At best, this could mean a long delay in the Rules Committee, and erosion of at least some Republican support for the bill on both sides of the Hill.

I added that we felt Halleck wouldn't have gone to the well on the bill without at least consulting Minority Leader Dirksen. Katzenbach promised he would do all he could to assuage our concerns. He said he felt that he had a good rapport with Senator Dirksen and that because the Senate was a smaller body than the House, communication might be easier. We agreed to keep in touch.

A little later, Bill Phillips of the Democratic Study Group called to find out whether House Republicans had agreed to join the DSG in putting supportive statements of church leaders in the Congressional Record, where House and Senate proceedings were reported and members could preserve written material for the record. I had been instructed to tell him our answer was "not yet"—not until bipartisan support was solidified.

At 3:30 p.m., I talked with Joe Sullivan of the *Wall Street Journal*, who said he was preparing a lengthy piece on how the bill got so badly fouled up and who was to blame.

At 3:45 p.m., reporter John Lindsay of *Newsweek* called, saying he'd been referred to me by the Rep. John Lindsay. He wanted to know what actually had happened in the Hotel Congressional meeting in room 410.

From 4:15 p.m. to 5:30 p.m., I joined Republican staff member Frederick Sontag in an off-the-record background meeting with nationally syndicated columnist Roscoe Drummond. Sontag hit away at the GOP's failure to get its message out on both civil rights and the Tom Curtis–John Lindsay initiative of 1962, which had been key to current developments. He also seemed sensitive to Halleck's concerns.

Diane Le Baker's suggestion of an analysis of Republican contributions seemed like a good idea.

* * *

The next day, November 1, I drafted an analysis showing House Judiciary Republican input to the bill. Meanwhile, Department of Justice attorneys joined Judiciary Committee staff Bill Foley, Herb Fuchs, and Benjamin Zelenko to begin preparing the Judiciary Committee's majority report.

The rules of Congress required that the Civil Rights Bill—H.R. 7152—be accompanied by a committee report before it could be placed on the Union Calendar, making it eligible to receive a special order from the Rules Committee to allow the bill to be brought to the floor of the House.

A committee report had a number of purposes. First, it had to spell out exactly what changes the bill it accompanied would make in *existing* law. Second, it was supposed to explain in detail the provisions of the bill. Third, it was the committee's only official statement of the reasons for the bill. Fourth, it presented the arguments both for and against a particular bill and was therefore useful to the press and to members of Congress seeking information for speeches, statements, news releases, and newsletters. Finally, it provided the legislative history of the bill, to aid in its interpretation by the administrative officials whose task it would be to enforce its provisions, and by the courts that might be asked to weigh in on the bill's constitutionality and the meaning of disputed passages. All in all, a committee report was a very useful document.

On November 2, a confidential copy of a draft of the majority report was completed, typed up at the Department of Justice, and circulated to Celler and McCulloch. McCulloch asked me for a frank appraisal of this report. He said the committee was applying a great deal of pressure on him in order to get the report out as quickly as possible. He added that the committee seemed more concerned about how fast they could get the report out than about what the report actually said.

In the early evening of November 3, I told McCulloch I thought the draft of the majority report was inadequate. McCulloch said he agreed with my impressions and would ask the committee staff to improve it by removing some partisan statements and by offering a fuller documentation of the reasons for the bill. Copenhaver reached the same conclusion, calling the report "a joke."

By the end of the day on November 4, the Republican members of the House Judiciary Committee had seen the draft of the committee report. Most of them were convinced it was a generally useless document. All it did properly was describe the contents of the legislation. It completely failed to heed the other important purposes typically accomplished by a committee report.

The previous day, I had met with Andy Glass of the *Herald Tribune* for lunch. We had a candid discussion at Sherrill's Bakery on prospects for the bill and views on the draft of the majority report. When Glass's article appeared on November 4, it infuriated both the committee Democrats and the administration because it said that the Justice Department—rather than the Judiciary Committee itself—had actually written the committee report. They might have been annoyed to see this information in print, but no one was questioning the accuracy of Glass's article.

Roscoe Drummond understood Halleck's reason for negotiating with the administration and devoted his November 4 column to a defense of Halleck. Republican Reps. William Springer of Illinois and Fred Schwengel of Iowa registered their support of Halleck's action on civil rights by inserting the Drummond article in the Congressional Record.

By November 5, the analysis of the civil rights bill that Copenhaver and I had worked on, which showed how the Republicans had affected the product voted out of the House Judiciary Committee, was ready for release. Its primary purpose was to catalogue Republican contributions to the bill. Its theme was that a host of changes were wrought in the bill upon Republican demand and would not have occurred without the insistence of the Judiciary Republicans backed by their House leadership.

No one seemed to take me seriously when I said we had written the analysis to quell a major revolt in the Republican ranks, which could threaten the bill's progress through the House. I argued that it was better we absorb some heat now in order to ensure at a later time the support of the overwhelming majority of the House Republicans. Without that support, the bill would have a very rough journey through the House.

Among the Republican members who were strong supporters of civil rights legislation, the hostile reaction to the criticism of the document was predictable. As a result, Lindsay's office (in the absence of Lindsay, who was in Europe at a NATO Parliamentarians' Conference) got rid of all its copies of the analysis. Other liberal Republican offices took similar steps.

Yet among some of the more conservative Republicans, the document was a smashing success. It was precisely what they and their constituents seemed to be looking for: an indication that the bill was not as strong as some had feared, but more important, a sign that Republicans had played a major role in shaping the legislation. This, the document provided. It therefore admirably fulfilled the purpose Copenhaver and I had set for it. Some offices requested many thousands of copies. When the supply dwindled, we gave them our permission to make copies of it for their own use. Many did just that.

In the middle of the furor, on November 7, McCulloch returned from a trip to his home state. After taking some soundings on the reception of the analysis, he ordered a halt to its distribution. Although he was well aware of the overwhelmingly positive response it had received from most House Republican members, he thought it had accomplished its purpose. Any further circulation of it could only harm the Republican civil rights position. At any rate, he told me he felt it was being misinterpreted.

Throughout this period, southern congressmen expressed their amazement at the House Judiciary Republicans for having missed a golden opportunity to reap political capital on the bill. The response of Representative Robert Ashmore, Democrat of South Carolina, was typical. During breakfast at the House cafeteria on November 5 with Marion Clow, Rep. Lindsay's administrative assistant, and me, Representative Ashmore shook his head sadly when he spoke of his surprise at the failure of Lindsay and other liberals to put the administration on the spot. He said we had everything to gain and nothing to lose by sticking with the Moore motion.

Rep. Ashmore further said that he and the other southerners knew that some kind of bill was sure to come out of the committee. They had been resigned to this fact for some time, yet had hoped for a more moderate bill. Their anger at the way the substitute was forced through the committee would have never manifested itself if the committee had taken three or four weeks for an orderly attempt to discuss and amend the substitute.

Moreover, Ashmore indicated his belief that the tactics of the majority of the Judiciary Committee might delay the bill longer in the end, because a large number of southern congressmen who might have remained silent would now be certain to request an opportunity to testify before the Rules Committee. This would further lessen the likelihood of early House consideration for a vote, as the Rules Committee would set the terms for the debate on the House floor—such as the number of hours and whether amendments would be allowed.

That week, as I was walking through the subway to the Capitol with Rep. Dick Poff, the Virginia Republican said that he thought the extreme and precipitous actions of the Judiciary Committee would create a climate where moderate southerners like him would be forced into more extreme positions. He said that dilatory tactics to slow the bill's progress were more likely now. A moderate bill handled in a reasonable fashion would have made passage of civil rights legislation a good deal easier.

Poff said he hoped that McCulloch and Lindsay recognized the value of keeping the fight going as far into next year as possible. He said this would help pick up Republican seats in the South, and would demonstrate to the North the incompetence of the administration and northern Democrats in getting their program through Congress.

On the afternoon of Monday, November 11, I had a long talk with Rep. McCulloch, who said that he continued to receive a lot of criticism over the Republican analysis. He still felt that its explanation of the Republican contributions had been misunderstood. He thought the tempo of the bill's journey through the legislative process would have to be slowed down.

"We erred considerably in forcing the compromise through the committee without allowing adequate opportunity for discussion and amendments," he admitted. "I did not make the decision to proceed in that fashion, but I should have resisted it more strongly."

McCulloch went on to say that at the other extreme, the Department of Justice had accused him of dragging his feet. "My reply to them, Bob," he said, "is that they've had their hand in too much of what has been done on the Hill." As he pointed out, the Justice Department was still very angry over the *Herald Tribune* story that had revealed its involvement in writing the committee report. "They did not like having it known that they were doing the work of our committee. It embarrassed them."

I told McCulloch that I had spoken to Glass, and that I had done so to reduce some of the secrecy around the bill and to relieve some of the pressure on the Republicans to sign off on the majority report. I asked him how many votes we would lose on the bill if we continued trying to push it through the House as rapidly as possible.

McCulloch replied that it might be more than we could afford. "There are times when we must move with speed, and there are times when we must move with caution," he advised. "This, I fear, is a time for caution. Otherwise, our efforts may fail. Although we have problems, I am pleased, by and large, with the progress we have made." He said that the newspapers in Ohio had been kind regarding his efforts on bringing the bill out of the committee and produced a number of editorials and stories that spoke favorably of his work.

On November 13, Rep. Lindsay had just returned from Europe and thus had his first chance to read the draft of the majority report. He told Copenhaver and me that the report was so inadequate, he would feel derelict in his duty if he did not write separate views covering the many areas that the majority had omitted. The next day, November 14, Lindsay told me that the committee staff—which had set a November 18 deadline for the filing of all separate views—was trying to persuade him to sign the majority report. He said he told Bill Foley, committee counsel, the report was a disgrace.

I spoke with Bob Moses of SNCC on November 14 about the voting rights efforts in Mississippi. He asked me questions about the bill's legislative process. I also learned from Bob Allott, Minority Leader Halleck's administrative assistant, that Halleck felt things had quieted down and was now anxious to get the bill through the House as soon as possible. Allott said that Rules Committee Chairman Judge Smith, Democrat of Virginia, planned to use the Rules Committee hearings "to let people know what's in the bill."

Copenhaver and I continued to work on the separate—additional—views of some Republican committee members, which would accompany the majority report. Separate views allowed committee members to offer their own perceptions about a bill's purpose, provisions, and impact, and why they voted for or against the bill. Copenhaver was near the breaking point, as he was assisting Meader, King, Moore, and Martin in the writing of their additional views and also had assumed the major task of aiding Cramer and Poff in the framing of the southern Republican position.

For his part, when delivering an address on November 15 at the AFL-CIO convention in New York City,

President Kennedy spoke of "our bill" and of the great progress his administration had made in the field of civil rights. This was hardly evidence of the bipartisanship for which we had hoped.

During those days, my friends on the Hill and elsewhere were either quitting or being fired, working too hard or not working enough, complaining too much over very little or stoically bearing harsh treatment and indifference. It was a very frustrating time, compounded by the pressure so many of us felt about securing the passage of the civil rights bill. The week beginning Monday, November 18, was the most depressing and disheartening week of all.

Copenhaver and I had worked hard, but to no avail. We failed to finish the separate views in time for inclusion in the committee report. No one besides Lindsay had given us much encouragement; some of the committee members seemed indifferent to the writing of separate views.

When the committee report was filed on November 20, it contained a majority report that satisfied very few, along with separate views—across the political spectrum—from Robert Kastenmeier, George Meader, Carlton King, Arch Moore, the southern Democrats, the southern Republicans, and William Cramer, but not from liberal Republicans.

By the afternoon of November 20, Lindsay had received the support of liberal Republicans MacGregor, Cahill, Bromwell, and Mathias for the submission of their additional views with his. Yet we learned that the additional views could not be submitted to the House now without the unanimous approval of all the representatives.

I spoke with Bill Brown, the assistant parliamentarian to Lew Deschler, who had been House parliamentarian since 1928. Brown explained that Lindsay would have to make a unanimous consent request in order to file the additional views, but in order to ensure the granting of the request, he would have to check first with Deschler and House Speaker McCormack.

This confirmed what was well known in the House—the pivotal role played by Lew Deschler in many of its key decisions. For if Lindsay did not check first with Parliamentarian Deschler when seeking recognition on the floor to submit additional views, McCormack would turn to Deschler and inquire if he knew why Lindsay was on his feet seeking recognition. If Lindsay had not spoken first with Deschler, the congressman might not even be recognized. If he were recognized, however, the Speaker might pause long enough to alert a southerner who might then object.

The House adjourned on Thursday, November 21, before Lindsay could reach the floor. The request would have to be delayed until after the weekend. Lindsay did manage, however, to clear his request with Deschler, who relayed word of it to Speaker McCormack.

The reaction by the House Republicans to the committee's majority report was so unfavorable that McCulloch decided that day to prepare his own separate Republican views. It was not clear at this time whether he was aware of what Lindsay and the others were planning, but he might have been. What McCulloch envisioned, however, was a more modest statement than Lindsay was contemplating—something that moderate Republican representatives like Garner Shriver, William Miller, Carlton King, and McCulloch himself could be comfortable with.

But of course, the next day was November 22, 1963.

CHAPTER 16

Tragedy and Trouble
November 22–December 18, 1963

Few people alive that Friday, November 22, could ever forget where they were when President John F. Kennedy was assassinated while riding in an open car through the streets of Dallas. The world shared the calamity, but each person endured his own private hell on that day and for many days to come.

I remember the few occasions I had met Kennedy in the fall of 1957 when he was a senator from Massachusetts. He and Mrs. Kennedy, staying in New York City while expecting the birth of their first child, Caroline, lived in the apartment directly above my family's. In the elevator, he would tease me, saying that his high school used to "kick your ass" in football. He was witty and quick in conversation.

The terrible news of his assassination came over the ticker tape in the Republican Congressional Committee office, which was across the hall from my RLRA office in the Hotel Congressional. We had been preparing to issue a press release that day, blasting the administration for breaking the spirit of bipartisan accord on civil rights. I immediately stopped the distribution of the release before it was issued and ordered all copies destroyed.

Most people in the vicinity of my office were genuinely grief-stricken, but a few thought we should get back to business as usual. Some even said the event—the assassination—was inevitable. One said it could damage Republican chances in the coming election.

I was sick at heart at this kind of talk. To me, in the face of so unspeakable a tragedy, everything had paled into insignificance. Suddenly, Washington was an unbearably depressing place to be. The following morning, I left the city.

* * *

I did not return to Washington until a week later—November 29. Two days before that, Rep. Lindsay had made his unanimous consent request to file additional views before the close of the day's session on December 2. Lindsay spoke on behalf of himself, Cahill, Bromwell, Mathias, and MacGregor. The national tragedy fortified Republican supporters of the bill to bring out their underlying reasons for the legislation in their additional views accompanying the committee report. Kennedy's assassination convinced me, as perhaps nothing else could, that we had done the right thing in reaching agreement with the administration.

Also, on November 27, President Johnson spoke powerfully to a joint session of Congress. "All I have," he said, "I would have given gladly not to be standing here today. . . . No memorial oration or eulogy could more eloquently honor President Kennedy's memory than the earliest possible passage of the civil rights bill for which he fought so long." Many people on both sides of the aisle believed President Johnson could help defuse some of the partisanship that had so frequently delayed the progress of the legislation.

Bill Copenhaver and I worked feverishly throughout the weekend to complete the additional views and thus offer a fuller explanation of the bill. We managed to get a complete draft of the document to Rep. Lindsay in installments during Saturday afternoon and Sunday morning, with the help of Copenhaver's assistant Karen Cuddy; Stuart Huseby from Rep. Schwengel's office; Madeleine McCarty, Marian Clow, and Judy Sandy from Lindsay's office; and especially Mary Kelley from MacGregor's office. Lindsay made a number of suggestions and changes, and the document was finished by Sunday night.

On Monday, November 30, after distributing copies to the committee members who planned to sign it, I went to McCulloch's office and showed him a copy as a matter of courtesy. McCulloch asked who was planning to go along with it. I told him Lindsay and his four colleagues. He then asked me if the members had wanted him to join them. I said I was sure they would be very happy if he thought the document was worthy of his support. He then spent the rest of the day going over the statement of their views with as much thoroughness as it is possible to imagine.

The other members were quick to sign the report. But McCulloch took his time. It was only minutes before the House adjourned when he and Rep. Shriver decided to join the original five. Shriver said simply, "I'm signing. I've got to go home." McCulloch and I sat on the House floor until they turned the lights off in the chamber, as McCulloch made last-minute changes that finally satisfied him. Only then did he sign.

It was worth the wait. His support of the views gave the document greater credibility than it otherwise would have had. With McCulloch's weighty perspective, the report would be received as an indication of Republican leadership sentiment.

For his part, Rep. Miller, the Republican National Committee chairman, flatly refused to sign any report. And Minority Leader Halleck asked Rep. McCulloch if a statement could be added indicating that the under-signed—Halleck—reserved the right to oppose the FEPC title when the bill reached the floor. Lindsay and McCulloch talked Halleck out of this. They argued that it would be better for the Republicans to maintain a flexible position, which would strengthen their bargaining stance later on.

With the holiday season upon us, much time and energy were expended in a debate between the Democrats and the Republicans over the best way to bring the civil rights bill to the floor of the House. The House Democrats, led by Rep. Bolling of Missouri, favored the use of the discharge petition, which—if signed by a majority of the House membership—would discharge the Rules Committee from further consideration of H.R. 7152. This would then free the civil rights bill to go directly to the House floor.

The Republicans preferred a potentially faster Calendar Wednesday procedure, which would likewise allow the House Judiciary Committee to bypass the Rules Committee to bring the measure directly to the House floor.

Neither plan, however, was successful or even workable.

* * *

At 1:00 p.m. on December 4, a meeting of the Leadership Conference on Civil Rights got underway at the Hotel Mayflower in downtown Washington. The meeting was of special importance, as the NAACP's Roy Wilkins; Walter Reuther, president of the United Automobile Workers (UAW); and other national leaders of groups participating in the Leadership Conference were to be in attendance. The purpose of the gathering was to map future strategy in regard to the civil rights bill. Democratic Rep. Richard Bolling was scheduled to speak.

I was notified of the meeting by SNCC's Bill Higgs, who thought the Republicans should have a representative at the gathering even though none had been invited. I told Reps. McCulloch, Lindsay, and Curtis of the meeting, and the invitation I had received from Higgs. All three urged me to attend and report back to them afterwards.

To avoid what I thought might be a problem for me—a lone Republican staff member showing up unexpectedly—I asked Kent Watkins, the administrative assistant to Democratic Representative William Moorhead of Pennsylvania, to come with me. He readily agreed to do so.

We arrived at the Mayflower a few minutes before the meeting began and quickly learned that our presence (primarily, my presence) was unwelcome. Marvin Caplan and Violet Gunther, representing the Leadership Conference, informed us that we would not be permitted to sit in on the meeting.

Higgs was upset by this, as were John Pemberton and Larry Speiser of the American Civil Liberties Union, James Hamilton of the National Council of Churches, and Walter Fauntroy of the Southern Christian Leadership Conference. Pemberton, the ACLU's national director, carried our request for admission to Joe Rauh.

Rauh denied our admission on the grounds that the day's meeting was closed; only Bolling, who was scheduled to speak, had been invited. Rauh said he assumed everyone knew there would be no visitors allowed at the session. Pemberton, Hamilton, and Higgs all denied being informed of a prohibition of that sort.

I asked Rauh why no Republican members of Congress had been invited to a meeting of such importance. He replied that he thought an invitation had been extended to Rep. Brown, but Brown had sent his regrets. Later, I learned that this was not quite accurate. Rep. Bolling had merely asked Brown what he could tell the group on Brown's behalf, knowing that Brown could not be present at the meeting. No one thought to invite a Republican in Brown's place, except the conference members who were trying to secure my presence as an observer.

A final appeal on my behalf was made to Rauh and Clarence Mitchell, who said they would ask Roy Wilkins. Rauh and Wilkins then spoke briefly with Walter Reuther, who had just entered the ballroom. Rauh returned with the final word. We could not stay. That was it.

That discussion revealed the extent to which the Leadership Conference's decisions were shaped by the UAW's Walter Reuther. It was Reuther and Rauh, and not the elected heads of the Leadership Conference, who made the decision to bar me from the meeting. In fact, it was Rauh, counsel to the UAW, who made many of the conference's key decisions.

In general, the unions exercised political influence on the conference. To the question of what was of greater importance, the Democratic Party or the civil rights movement, the union chieftain unhesitatingly would answer the former—the party. This close alliance between unions and the national Democratic Party often influenced the civil rights groups to move in directions deliberately and necessarily calculated to embarrass Republicans. This kind of narrow partisanship did not help the chances of passing the best possible civil rights bill.

As I headed back through the lobby of the Mayflower, I ran into Ned Kenworthy of the *New York Times* and Andy Glass of the *New York Herald Tribune*, whom

Watkins and I had joined for lunch earlier. They asked why I was leaving the meeting before it began. When I told them what had happened, they were astonished. I said I hoped the incident at the Mayflower would not be reported. In public, at least, we needed to maintain a united bipartisan front.

Rep. Lindsay was on the House floor when I reached him by telephone. He said that Rauh could have gotten us in if he'd wanted to. Lindsay then spoke with Glass and Kenworthy about the incident. They all agreed this kind of occurrence made it difficult to maintain a united bipartisan coalition in support of the bill.

H.R. 7152 was now awaiting a "rule" from the Rules Committee for governing the bill's debate on the House floor. There was concern that Rep. Smith—the committee's chairman and a conservative southern Democrat from Virginia whose segregationist views were well known—would find ways to bog down the current bill in the committee as he had done with previous civil rights legislation.

On December 5, Charlie Halleck had breakfast with President Johnson at the White House. Upon returning to the Hill, Rep. Halleck told reporters what he had promised the president: that the Rules Committee Republicans would do everything possible to get the bill out of the committee after about two weeks of hearings. That same day, Chairman Smith announced that hearings on the bill would begin, as the *New York Times* reported on December 6, "reasonably soon in January." Halleck expressed surprise when he heard about Chairman Smith's plans, but noted that if Smith said he would begin hearings then, his word could be counted on.

Some observers believed the threat of a discharge petition, which would have allowed the bill to bypass the Rules Committee and go directly to the House floor, prompted Smith's announcement. However, it was more likely a result of Smith's consultations with Clarence Brown, the ranking Republican committee member—a conservative but, unlike Smith, a proponent of civil rights legislation.

Both Smith and Brown—Democrat and Republican—sincerely felt, in my view, that the bill was too emotion-charged and controversial to be rushed through the House with parliamentary shortcuts and lacking input on the terms of debate from the Rules Committee. But they also seemed to believe genuinely that bringing the bill to the floor without undue delay was essential.

The *New York Times'* perceptive December 6 account by Ned Kenworthy conveyed the swift-moving events and complex maneuvering that had reached a climax of sorts with Smith's announcement heralding the approximate start of Rules Committee hearings on the bill.

> Today was a day of general peacemaking and face-saving, and it had its amusing moments as everybody came away with something to show from a fracas that left everything as it had been at the outset.
>
> The Republican leadership was happy because it had won its battle to preserve orderly procedure while assuring that the bill would reach the floor "after reasonable hearings," as Mr. Halleck put it.

The Administration was both happy and relieved. When Republican tempers flared over the discharge petition, it became obvious that the necessary 60 Republican signatures would not be immediately forthcoming. Failure to get the signatures would have been an embarrassing defeat for President Johnson. That defeat was avoided.

But at the same time the Administration strategists could say that the threat of the petition had brought Mr. Smith to heel. And this claim, though of doubtful validity because the signatures were wanting, could be used effectively to convince civil rights groups that the President meant business when he called for "earliest possible" action on the bill.

Even Mr. Smith had reason to be satisfied. He had never said he would not hold hearings, but only that he would not hold them in December. And he made that stick.

Thus he could maintain to his constituents that he had fought the good fight and yielded only to superior strength.

Because of the northern Democrats' desire to wrest the bill out of the Rules Committee quickly, tensions remained high, taking a toll on good will, rational discourse, and the bipartisanship necessary to pass the bill.

On December 9, Celler filed a petition to discharge the bill from the Rules Committee. The discharge petition required the signatures of 218 representatives, a majority of the House—but without encouragement from Halleck and McCulloch, the 60 votes needed from Republicans were not forthcoming.

On December 11, a Wednesday, the Republicans tested the Democrats by daring them to extract the bill from the Rules Committee immediately with a Calendar Wednesday procedure. The Democratic majority leader, Rep. Albert of Oklahoma—a steadying, conciliatory force during this difficult period—managed to keep the peace that day with a motion to adjourn.

On the other hand, Kent Watkins's call to me about the liberal Democratic Study Group's decision to seek more consultation with Republican supporters of the civil rights bill seemed like a good sign. So did a call on December 13 from Wes Barthelmes, the able administrative assistant of Representative Edith Green, Democrat of Oregon. "I know the Republicans are unhappy about the approach to the discharge petition," he said. "Dick Bolling is aware we've got problems. He would like to meet with you to air mutual grievances and improve the climate for bipartisanship."

I called Rep. Bolling right away. He asked me to come to his office at 6:00 p.m. On my way there, I stopped to talk to McCulloch. He told me to impress upon Bolling the need for increased consultation.

Bolling was very hospitable and impressed me then, as he did many times afterwards, as a tough, articulate man of great intelligence. He readily admitted that things had gotten fouled up, blaming some of the confusion on the aftermath of Kennedy's assassination, when "people were too numb to function coherently." He also put some of the onus for the communications failure on Chairman Celler: Democratic Rep. Bolling had always kept Rep. Brown, his Republican colleague on the Rules Committee, fully informed. Thus, Bolling had assumed—wrongly, it turned out—that Celler was keeping McCulloch and Lindsay similarly informed of the discharge plan.

I replied that all we knew, we had learned from the papers, cloakroom scuttlebutt, and informal contacts on the staff level.

Bolling regretted this. He said he would consult with Brown, McCulloch, and Lindsay in working out the timetable for bringing the bill to the floor. He hoped the Republicans would commit themselves to getting the bill out of the Rules Committee and onto the floor by the end of January.

He also outlined what he thought should be the procedure for handling the bill when it reached the House floor. Here, he placed great emphasis on a system the DSG was planning to set up so enough House members would be on the floor to forestall defeat on opposition amendments if the teller vote—when representatives would simply walk past a teller to be counted—was close. Since no record was kept of teller votes, members were known to skip them, and their constituents would be none the wiser.

The discussion ranged over other matters, from the crucial role of Lew Deschler in running the House to a book that Bolling was writing to his admiration for McCulloch. We parted amicably.

On December 18, Chairman Smith announced that the Rules Committee would start hearings on the civil rights bill on January 9. The chairman was going to have his "reasonably soon in January" hearings after all.

CHAPTER 17

From the Rules Committee to the House Floor to Passage in the Senate

January 9–July 2, 1964

On Thursday, January 9, 1964, the House of Representatives Committee on Rules met at 10:30 a.m. in room H-313 of the Capitol Building, Honorable Howard W. Smith, chairman, presiding.

The Chairman. The committee will be in order. Mr. Celler, there is a rumor around that you want to get a rule on H.R. 7152.

Mr. Celler. I confirm the rumor.

With these words, the House Rules Committee began hearings on the civil rights bill. Over the course of nine days (January 9, 14–16, 21–23, 28–29), the committee heard testimony on H.R. 7152 from 34 members of Congress and received statements from five others.

As I recall, the hearings ranged over a wide variety of subjects: busing, Civil Rights Commission inquiries into private group memberships, mob rule, the impossibility of legislating morality, the bill's cost to the taxpayer, jury trials, preemption, religion, chiropodists, Native Americans, secret votes on the floor, the meaning of desegregation, a Human Rights Resettlement Commission, the Mann Act, Prohibition, sex, Trojan horses, record-keeping, rumors, deals, labels, slogans, points of order, fairness, bankers, church socials, honest men, the Taft–Hartley Act, and the states of Ohio and Indiana— and some serious statements too on when the hearings would end, the contents of the legislation, and the bill's significance to the American people.

Along the way, Rep. Judge Smith, the Rules Committee chairman, professed concern about what he called "booby traps" in the bill, as he tried to lead its supporters into tight places in their defense of the legislation. One of the most amusing moments of the hearings was the colloquy between Chairman Smith and Rep. McCulloch.

Smith tried vainly to secure from McCulloch a full revelation of what had occurred in the execution session of the House Judiciary Committee on October 29, 1963, when the substitute bill was approved. McCulloch, for his part, told Smith that in an effort to comply with the House rules, both he and Chairman Celler had spoken for just one minute. Smith's next question elicited the most memorable exchange of the hearings:

> **The Chairman.** How did you get to be favored with all of that time of one minute?
>
> **Mr. McCulloch.** Because of my receding red hair.
>
> **The Chairman.** I would like to state that is about as good a reason as I have heard.

Perhaps the most eloquent, searching moments of the hearings came at the close of McCulloch's testimony on January 15, when Democrat Carl Elliott of Alabama and McCulloch, two of the most compassionate of men, had a rewarding discussion on some of the difficult problems of the bill. Hope, fear, promise, and uncertainty were mingled in a moving commentary on the relation of civil rights to the future of America.

I attended all the hearings, and by the time they were over, I knew where Chairman Smith would focus his attention during the debate on the House floor: on Title I (voting) and Title II (public accommodations). As I told McCulloch and Lindsay, if they were prepared on those portions of the bill, the southerners would likely run out of steam during debate and amendments on the rest of the measure.

On January 30, the House Rules Committee approved a rule clearing the civil rights bill for floor debate starting the next day. The vote was 11–4: four southern Democrats—Smith, Elliott, William Colmer of Mississippi, and James Trimble of Arkansas—voted against the rule, which provided that after 10 hours of general debate, the bill would be read by title and open to amendments under the five-minute rule, allowing representatives to speak multiple times but limited to five minutes at a time.

Ten hours of general debate at the start was a somewhat shorter allocation than the southerners—and, in fact, Celler and McCulloch—had originally wanted. But Chairman Smith agreed to it in exchange for a guarantee that the southerners would have a full opportunity under the five-minute rule to make their fight against the bill. No effort would be made to shut off the proceedings until February 11, which was deemed an adequate amount of time for amendments and debate. Smith also promised that if the agreement were kept, the southerners would not resort to dilatory tactics.

During that afternoon, the southern caucus, chaired by Rep. Colmer, convened (appropriately enough) in the Caucus Room of the Cannon House Office Building. About 60 members from all southern states attended the strategy session. One non-southerner, John Lindsay of New York, also received an invitation—by mistake. Rather than embarrass his southern colleagues openly, Lindsay returned the invitation to Rep. Willis of Louisiana, and the two shared a good laugh about it.

"You might as well come," Willis said to Lindsay. "It isn't going to matter much what kind of strategy we plan. You and I know how this fight is going to end." Lindsay thanked Willis but declined his offer.

After one of the Rules Committee hearings, Chairman Smith spoke to me in the corridor. Echoing what Willis had told Lindsay, Smith said there wasn't much the southern members of Congress could do to stop this bill. "You're going to have to run over us," admitted the 80-year-old Smith. "This is painful for me. I would have been happier if one of the younger members had taken on the leadership of this fight, but that was not to be."

Judge Smith was almost universally admired for his ability to direct and shape legislation, even if many of those admirers disagreed with his views. I considered him the most skilled and brilliant legislator of his time. The manner in which he exercised his power as chairman of the Rules Committee won the respect of even those members on the committee who were his strongest opponents.

* * *

The debate on the House floor began on Friday, January 31, when Speaker McCormack recognized Representative Ray Madden, a member of the Rules Committee. The Indiana Democrat called up House Resolution 616, which provided the guidelines for debate on the civil rights bill, and asked for its immediate consideration.

The clerk read the resolution, and Rep. Clarence Brown, the ranking Republican on the Rules Committee, opened debate. Brown told his colleagues that an agreement had been reached by the leadership on both sides of the aisle not to cut off debate on the bill under the five-minute rule "until and unless every Member of the House who may desire to do so will have the full opportunity to offer and to discuss any amendment that he may wish to submit for consideration." Brown hoped that by avoiding unnecessary quorum calls and filibuster tactics, "this House will demonstrate to the world that legislation of this importance . . . is being considered prayerfully, justly, and fully."

Brown concluded eloquently:

> If I may, I would like to appeal to the Membership of the House for cooperation to that end, regardless of whether you are for or against the bill, for or against any amendment or any change in it, that we do conduct this debate on a high plane, that we can at least say to our children and to our grandchildren, we participated in one of the great debates of modern American history and we did it as statesmen and not as quarreling individuals.

A short time later, the resolution to bring H.R. 7152 to the floor was adopted by a voice vote. Chairman Celler rose and was recognized by the Speaker.

> **Mr. Celler.** Mr. Speaker, I move that the House resolve itself into the Committee of the Whole House on the State of the Union for the consideration of the bill (H.R. 7152) . . .

The Motion was agreed to.

Accordingly, the House resolved itself into the Committee of the Whole . . . with Mr. Keogh in the chair.

The Clerk read the title of the bill.

By unanimous consent, the first reading of the bill was dispensed with.

The Committee of the Whole House on the State of the Union, also known as the Committee of the Whole, referred to the House membership sitting as a committee made up of the entire House. It was an ancient parliamentary institution—a creation of the English Parliament. Most important legislation considered by the House of Representatives was considered in this manner.

Although the House itself required a quorum of 218 to do business, in the Committee of the Whole—whose primary function was to expedite legislative business—a quorum consisted of just 100. With the House sitting as the Committee of the Whole, a bill was first discussed under general debate and then considered for amendments under the five-minute rule. While the committee was in session, teller votes could be requested by just 20 members rather than by a full one-fifth of the House membership.

Unlike in regular sessions, the Speaker of the House did not preside over the Committee of the Whole. Instead, the presiding officer was an ordinary member chosen by the Speaker on the basis of his seniority, judgment, parliamentary skill, and, on crucial bills, the respect in which he was held by his colleagues.

Rep. Eugene Keogh of Brooklyn, New York, a congressman since 1936 and a powerful member of the tax-writing House Ways and Means Committee, was chosen by Speaker McCormack to be chairman of the Committee of the Whole during consideration of the civil rights bill. Many times over the years, he had been singled out by his colleagues as the best person for the job of chairman. A number of reasons were cited in Keogh's support. First, he was a sagacious, experienced veteran who knew his way around and would not get rattled when the going got tough. Second, he was an outstanding legislator—a man who could get things done. Third, he had friends and contacts on both sides of the aisle as well as on both sides of the Mason–Dixon Line. With Keogh in the chair, the southerners would accept as a given that they would receive a fair shake.

Finally, Keogh had a good voice, a commanding presence, a jaunty air, a sense of humor, and a matchless ability to obtain order during the debate by securing prompt obedience to his impressive delivery of the magic parliamentary words: "The gentleman will suspend. All members will please clear the aisles. Those wishing to converse will retire to the cloakrooms. The gentleman from [name of state]."

The debate on H.R. 7152—colorful, intense, and lengthy as it was—provided few surprises. One occurred when Democratic Rep. Byron Rogers offered an amendment to extend the life of the Civil Rights Commission for four years, thus breaking the agreement the Republicans had fought for with the administration to make the commission permanent. Although the Republicans believed permanent extension would ensure the commission's independence from the White House and Justice

Department, McCulloch and Lindsay knew there was no point in opposing the Rogers amendment. The united support of the Democrats would assure its adoption anyway, and McCulloch and Lindsay felt it would be better not to air the partisan disagreement any further on the House floor. The administration thus achieved what it had long sought.

A second moment of drama occurred on the seventh day of debate, during consideration of Title VI, related to the withholding of federal funds from discriminatory programs. It was at Title VI that the southerners made their last, determined stand against the bill.

Democratic Representative Oren Harris of Arkansas, chairman of the Interstate Commerce Committee, offered a so-called perfecting amendment, meant to "perfect"—with insertions, deletions, or both—an amendment under consideration. In this case, Representative Harris sought to bring back the language for Title VI from the original Kennedy administration bill, which would have dispensed with mandatory withholding of federal funds from programs that practiced discrimination, given the president discretionary authority instead, and eliminated judicial review in instances where funding was cut off. His amendment would have weakened Title VI—and pleased southern Democrats.

After Representative Hale Boggs, the Democratic whip from Louisiana, spoke in favor of the amendment, Lindsay rose to reply. Clearly outraged, he assailed the amendment. He had already sent a congressional page to alert McCulloch—who was conferring off the House floor with

Halleck, Albert, and McCormack—about the situation. Returning to the chamber, McCulloch spoke briefly with Lindsay, then hurried across the floor to Celler. I could see all this from my seat in the gallery next to Mrs. McCulloch and the McCullochs' daughter Nancy.

Only a few minutes before, Roy Wilkins had come into the gallery to say hello to Mrs. McCulloch. Wilkins told her how grateful everyone was for the great work her husband was doing. She told him how pleased she was to meet him. It was not an easy encounter for her, as in 1960 Wilkins had sent telegrams to the NAACP in Lima, Ohio, asking for McCulloch's defeat in the congressional election and calling him a "double-crosser" because he could not support all the demands of the Leadership Conference on Civil Rights. Now they needed McCulloch desperately, however, for without his support, their task would be many times more difficult.

When McCulloch left Celler and headed back to the Republican side, Mrs. McCulloch gently tugged my arm and exclaimed, "Bill's mad! I know it because his neck is red. It always gets red when he's really upset."

Indeed, McCulloch grabbed the microphone at the committee table and, in a voice quivering with emotion, asked Rep. Meader, who had the floor, to yield to him. McCulloch spoke with more fervor and deliberation than I could ever remember hearing him express:

> If we pick up this old provision from the bill which did not get consideration and which does not provide for judicial review, I regret to say that my individual support of the legislation will come to an end.

Having already conceded on a four-year extension in place of a permanent Civil Rights Commission, McCulloch was livid about another attempt to modify the bill. McCulloch's dramatic statement rocked the chamber. Across the floor, near the door to the Democratic cloakroom, Majority Leader Albert looked dumbfounded. Rep. Thompson of New Jersey, one of the coordinators for House Democrats on the bill, rushed from the chamber to confer with administration officials. Speaker McCormack headed straight toward Celler. But there was no need for him to do so. Celler was on his feet seeking recognition. He knew what had to be done.

Speaking in a clear voice that could be heard throughout the vast expanse of the House chamber, Celler told his colleagues, "I am unalterably opposed to the amendment offered by the gentleman from Arkansas."

That settled it. I couldn't help wondering, however, whether the Democratic whip Boggs had spoken in support of the Harris amendment because of an agreement with the administration or because it was a southern effort to modify the bill—or both.

Sen. Thompson had been hard at work gathering up northern Democrats, who now poured onto the House floor. The amendment was going to be slaughtered.

Chairman Keogh put the question on the Harris amendment. Representative Harris demanded tellers. The vote was, indeed, overwhelming. The tellers reported that the amendment had been defeated 80–206.

A critical moment had passed.

The next day, the women of the House of Representatives—notably silent during the debate—rose to speak when Chairman Smith made good on his word to Maine correspondent May Craig on *Meet the Press*: to do something about protecting the rights of women. Smith offered an amendment to prohibit discrimination in employment due not only to race, color, religion, and national origin—which were already covered under the title—but also to sex.

It was not obvious from the start that chivalry would win the day. In the end, the amendment passed with 168 representatives voting for it, but 133 against it. Still, it was a victory for women, and also for Chairman Smith—unless he was actually hoping to undermine and ultimately defeat the bill with his amendment. To be fair, though, there was evidence that he had championed women's rights in the past.

Two days later, on February 10—a day before the agreed-on deadline—debate ended with a vote just before 8:00 p.m. The bill finally passed, with 290 in favor and 130 against, with 11 not voting. Of those, 152 Democrats and 138 Republicans voted for the bill; 96 Democrats and 34 Republicans voted against it.

In retrospect, the Harris amendment would be considered the most serious threat to the bipartisan coalition supporting the bill of the entire floor debate. What had happened to bring Lindsay and McCulloch to their feet in such dramatic fashion? Why were they so certain that a problem had actually developed?

Afterwards, when queried by reporters, Rep. Boggs—whose presence and words had touched off the excitement—sharply denied that he was speaking for the Democratic leadership, the White House, or the Justice Department. He claimed he was speaking only for himself.

Or was he?

Probably not. Much later, when the question was discussed, three associates of House Democratic members shared something interesting with me: The night before Harris had offered his amendment, they had been informed that there might be an administration-backed move to soften the impact of Title VI. They had heard some talk that Boggs was part of it.

At the time of the incident on the floor, however, the Republicans were not aware of this information. Instead, they were simply bothered by some incidents that indicated the administration might be reneging on the October agreement. The move to cut back the life of the Civil Rights Commission had alerted them to the possibility that other such actions—perhaps like the Harris amendment—might be forthcoming.

What Lindsay and McCulloch did not know at that time, although they later claimed they had heard rumors to the effect, was that their instincts were much surer than they could have realized. For it is clear that such a weakening move, with the active participation of Boggs, had been contemplated. In acting as they did, McCulloch and Lindsay may have saved the bill from a greater crisis later.

* * *

From the House, H.R. 7152 went to the Senate, where—after four months of debate—the much-anticipated southern

Democrats' filibuster was finally broken and the bill passed on June 19, 1964, by a vote of 73–27. On July 2, President Lyndon Johnson signed the Civil Rights Act into law. Although Congress passed the Voting Rights Act of 1965 a year later, equal voting rights would still be a contentious issue in the 21st century. Even so, an important round in the ongoing civil rights struggle was over.

During the battle to pass the civil rights bill, the Republican Party and its national committee were being transformed gradually, though not subtly, into more conservative and southern organizations—more in harmony with the party's likely 1964 standard-bearer, Senator Barry Goldwater of Arizona. Moderate elected officials and staff members in Washington were being replaced by Goldwater loyalists.

Even before President Johnson signed the bill into law, Representative McCulloch and others were urging Bill Copenhaver and me to attend the Republican National Convention in San Francisco, which took place at the Cow Palace arena between July 13 and July 16. It was our responsibility to help McCulloch and other moderates, especially the Nelson Rockefeller liberal wing of the party (which was supporting the doomed candidacy of Pennsylvania Governor William Scranton for the presidential nomination) draft a strong civil rights plank for the Republican platform.

We tried, but our efforts were fruitless. The Platform Committee, dominated by Goldwater supporters, blocked even a moderate civil rights plank. The fight was carried to the convention floor, where a similar proposal was decisively defeated.

Representative William Miller of New York, the party's national committee chairman, who had been largely absent during the deliberations on the civil rights bill, had helped turn the party over to the Goldwater loyalists. He was in turn rewarded when Goldwater chose him to be his running mate in the 1964 presidential election.

A few months later, at the start of the 89th Congress in January 1965, Representative Charlie Halleck was replaced as minority leader by Representative Gerald Ford of Michigan. The vote against Halleck was close: 73–69. The main reason for Halleck's defeat was his vocal support for the civil rights bill.

1964 was a time of seismic change for the future of the Republican Party. For the Republicans who had worked so hard for the passage of civil rights legislation, it marked the beginning of a new, more entrenched political era. But they could look back with pride at the party's crucial role in the enactment of the historic Civil Rights Act.

The End

References

CHAPTER 3

Rep. Roosevelt/Rep. Lindsay excerpt from *Congressional Record, House of Representatives, 88th Congress, 1st Session* (September 17, 1963), US Government Printing Office: 17283.

CHAPTER 4

Rep. Celler excerpt from *Hearings Before the Committee on Rules, House of Representatives, 88th Congress, 2nd Session, on H.R. 7152* (January 14, 1964), US Government Printing Office: 164.

CHAPTER 5

Rep. Cramer excerpt from *Additional Individual Views of Hon. William C. Cramer on H.R. 7152, Committee on the Judiciary, House of Representatives, 88th Congress, 1st Session* (November 20, 1963), US Government Printing Office, Civil Rights Act of 1963 [sic].

Rep. Meader excerpt from *Additional Individual Views of Hon. George Meader on H.R. 7152, Committee on the Judiciary, House of Representatives, 88th Congress, 1st Session* (November 20, 1963), US Government Printing Office, Civil Rights Act of 1963 [sic].

CHAPTER 7

AG Kennedy testimony excerpts from *Hearings Before the Committee on the Judiciary, House of Representatives, 88th Congress, 1st Session, on H.R. 7152, as amended by Subcommittee No. 5* (October 15–16, 1963), US Government Printing Office: 2652, 2653,

2654, 2658, 2674, 2679, 2686, 2687, 2692, 2693, 2697, 2698, 2757, 2759, 2760, 2761.

CHAPTER 8

Excerpts from *Congressional Record, House of Representatives, 88th Congress, 1st Session* (October 17, 1963), US Government Printing Office: 19803–19805.

CHAPTER 9

Excerpts from "The Congress: Where Are We At Here?" *Time*, November 1, 1963. From TIME. ©1963 TIME USA LLC. All rights reserved. Used under license.

CHAPTER 12

Article by Anthony Lewis, "Congress Faces Crucial Decision on Civil Rights," the *New York Times*, October 28, 1963. From the *New York Times*. ©1963 The New York Times Company. All rights reserved. Used under license.

CHAPTER 16

Excerpts from E. W. Kenworthy, "Rights Bill Move Set for January," the *New York Times*, December 6, 1963. From the *New York Times*. ©1963 The New York Times Company. All rights reserved. Used under license.

CHAPTER 17

House Rules Committee excerpts from *Hearings Before the Committee on Rules, House of Representatives, 88th Congress, 2nd Session, on H.R. 7152* (January 9–29, 1964), U.S. Government Printing Office: 1, 211.

House of Representatives debate excerpts from *Congressional Record, House of Representatives, 88th Congress, 2nd Session* (January 31, 1964), US Government Printing Office: 1514, 1516.

Additional House of Representatives excerpt from *Congressional Record, House of Representatives, 88th Congress, 2nd Session* (February 7, 1964), US Government Printing Office: 2492.

Acknowledgments

I am immensely grateful to the many people without whom this book would not be in your hands today.

First, I would like to thank publishing consultant Lisa Weinert, who recommended Greenleaf Book Group/River Grove Books as a publisher for *Crisis and Compromise.*

Also deserving of my sincere appreciation is the entire Greenleaf team, including Justin Branch, who extended a warm welcome; Lindsay Bohls and Jessica Reyes, who shepherded the book through the many steps of the publishing process; Sheila Parr, who designed the striking, imaginative cover; and especially Elizabeth Brown and Amy Dorta McIlwaine, two superb editors who let no detail escape their scrutiny. This undoubtedly is a far better book than I could have imagined, thanks to their perceptive questions, astute suggestions, and determination to bring out the best in me and my writing.

And to my family, my gratitude knows no bounds—in general, for their loving presence in my life and, in particular now, for their role in the genesis of this book. With a lot of free time on my hands during the COVID-19 pandemic in 2020, I decided to revisit the manuscript I had started decades earlier about my experience working on the landmark 1964 Civil Rights Act. My idea was that my children and grandchildren might want to learn more someday about that important period and its formative impact on my life. As I reread what I had written, though, I couldn't help thinking that its message about the need for bipartisanship was as important for our rancorous and divisive times as it had been during the struggle for this civil rights legislation. So thank you, Philip, Emily, and Alexandra, and Miranda, James, Dylan, and Arden, for motivating me to dust off my dormant but not forgotten manuscript with its very relevant message for today's world. (And here's an extra shoutout to Philip for his advice on the project.)

Finally, my everlasting thanks to Abigail, my wife and (as our children like to say) the rock of our family, for encouraging me to put pen to paper again and publish this memoir. Without her unwavering support and indomitable spirit, there would be no *Crisis and Compromise*.

About the Author

As legislative assistant to Representative John Lindsay of New York and head of a new congressional support organization called the Republican Legislative Research Association (RLRA), Robert Kimball had the once-in-a-lifetime opportunity to play a role in the events preceding the passage of the 1964 Civil Rights Act.

While serving in Rep. Lindsay's office, Mr. Kimball—a 1961 Yale College graduate in American studies—participated in discussions about bills introduced in the House of Representatives, including civil rights legislation. In his RLRA position, he provided staff assistance to Republican members of the House of Representatives for the civil rights legislative effort and reached out to them personally to mobilize backing for the legislation. In October 1963, he was one of the four people who hammered out the bipartisan compromise that helped enable the civil rights bill to move forward in the House. This memoir is, to Mr. Kimball's knowledge, the first detailed account by an actual participant in these events—and a reminder of a time when the divisions between Republicans and

Democrats were bridgeable and the needs of the country could trump partisanship.

Although Mr. Kimball was supposed to enter Yale Law School in the fall of 1963, he deferred matriculation until the following year in order to continue working on what became the Civil Rights Act of 1964. He received a law degree from Yale in 1967, but never practiced law or worked in Washington again. Instead, he pursued his passion for American musical theater, becoming a recognized scholar in that field. He has written extensively about the Great American Songbook and its creators, and has edited or coedited the lyrics of Cole Porter, Ira Gershwin, Irving Berlin, Lorenz Hart, Frank Loesser, and Johnny Mercer for "The Complete Lyrics" series published by Knopf.

Mr. Kimball and his wife, both native New Yorkers, are longtime residents of New York City's midtown Manhattan, where they raised their son and daughter and continue to enjoy the city's abundant cultural offerings.

From left: Robert Kimball, Rep. John V. Lindsay, and Secretary of the Interior Stewart Udall, June 11, 1963. (Photo credit: US Department of Interior)